Aeschylus: *Libation Bearers*

Aeschylus: *Libation Bearers*

C. W. Marshall

Bloomsbury Academic
An imprint of Bloomsbury Publishing Plc

B L O O M S B U R Y
LONDON • OXFORD • NEW YORK • NEW DELHI • SYDNEY

Bloomsbury Academic

An imprint of Bloomsbury Publishing Plc

50 Bedford Square	1385 Broadway
London	New York
WC1B 3DP	NY 10018
UK	USA

www.bloomsbury.com

BLOOMSBURY and the Diana logo are trademarks of Bloomsbury Publishing Plc

First published 2017

British Library Cataloguing-in-Publication Data

A catalogue record for this book is available from the British Library.

ISBN:	HB:	978-1-4742-5507-3
	PB:	978-1-4742-5506-6
	ePDF:	978-1-4742-5509-7
	ePub:	978-1-4742-5508-0

Library of Congress Cataloging-in-Publication Data

A catalog record for this book is available from the Library of Congress.

Series: Companions to Greek and Roman Tragedy

Cover image © Paestan Red-Figure Neck Amphora. Digital image courtesy of the Getty's Open Content Program.

Typeset by Fakenham Prepress Solutions, Fakenham, Norfolk NR21 8NN for Hallie and Jonah

Contents

List of tables

Preface

Libation Bearers is an understudied play. One reason for this is the brilliant and comprehensive commentary that was published in 1986 by Alex Garvie. When I was a doctoral student, this was held up for me as a model for commentary writing in English, and it was for that reason that Mr Garvie was selected as the external examiner for my doctorate. The same year saw another commentary by A. Bowen, in the preface of which he confessed, 'I came to love *Choephori* above all other Greek plays, and to grieve at its neglect' (1986: vi). In the time since then, significant revisions of the text have been produced by Sommerstein (in the Loeb Classical Library) and West (providing a Teubner text), and their associated studies have done much to improve our understanding of the play as it survives, but there has not been wide critical engagement with the play.

This book is designed particularly to help readers without Greek to approach the play, and to set out some key points of interpretation for anyone approaching Aeschylus' drama, whether for the first time or returning as part of a regular pilgrimage to the *Oresteia*. It slips between Barbara Goward's 2005 companion to *Agamemnon* and Robin Mitchell-Boyask's 2009 companion to *Eumenides*. There is a vast bibliography on the *Oresteia*, and I can only point to some of it in the notes. On issues of controversy, I have argued for my position, and have shown how other possibilities change the answers given. My method privileges theatrical performance as a means of interpreting a dramatic work. This is not the only approach, but it is one I have found helpful and which is especially important for works that are not in the active performance repertoire, such as *Libation Bearers*. Standards of functional literacy even in Athens were far below what we would consider acceptable in society today, and we must resist any urge towards logocentrism, privileging the words of the script without considering other elements of a play: for most Athenians in the fifth century BCE, *Libation Bearers* was a performance. Starting with performance and the practical questions it raises is therefore both healthy as a corrective and brings us closer to the experience of the initial spectators – a gulf that can only be crossed with effort, and even then incompletely.

I am grateful for support above all to my wife, Hallie Rebecca Marshall, who gives me so much. I taught the play at the University of British Columbia in 2014, and I thank Heather Odell particularly for her help afterwards. The Avarua Fishing Club was particularly conducive to productivity. Some ideas on the play were presented at the University of Manitoba in 2015, with thanks to Lea Stirling, Mike Sampson, and Mark Joyal. I am also grateful to Ian Storey, who is always generous with his time. Alice Wright and her team at Bloomsbury Academic have been amazingly patient and helpful. Part of this research has been supported by the Social Sciences and Humanities Research Council of Canada and the Peter Wall Institute for Advanced Studies at the University of British Columbia.

The book is dedicated to Hallie and Jonah, mother and son.

Conventions of spelling, etc.

Greek terms are italicized, and I try to transliterate terms consistently. The Greek alphabet has seven vowels, and the long e and o of eta and omega are marked as $\bar{e}$ and $\bar{o}$, to distinguish them from the short vowels epsilon and omicron (*e, o*). Upsilon (*u*) is transliterated as *u* or *y*, depending on euphony. A gamma before another consonant (*–gg–* or *–gk–*) is transliterated with an *n*, as in *angelos*. Proper names are given in their most common and accessible English form (e.g. Aeschylus, not Aiskhylos), with one exception. This practice does especial harm to the name of the queen: in Greek she is *Klytaimēstra* ('Famous for Plotting'), and so I have transliterated her name Clytaemestra instead of the more familiar Clytemnestra, a form found in Latin and medieval Greek, but not before.

Line references to the *Oresteia* use abbreviations for the play titles: *Agamemnon* (*Ag.*), *Libation Bearers* (*LB*), and *Eumenides* (*Eum.*).

All three-figure dates are BCE unless noted.

1

Theatre and Theodicy

Libation Bearers is a tragedy that depicts a young man murdering his mother because he believes the gods have told him to do so. In attempting to avenge his father's killing, Orestes brings himself to commit an act more horrific than the crime it answers, and the choice he makes will leave him polluted because he has shed family blood. It is a dark play with a surprise ending, and is theatrically aggressive in many ways. The play is named for the initial entry of the chorus, as twelve slave women appear carrying liquid ritual offerings to the grave of the Greek hero Agamemnon, who was himself murdered. In Greek, they are *Choēphoroi*, carriers of *choes*, a type of pouring vessel used in funeral offerings. The chorus is therefore composed of women bringing liquid offerings to a tomb.

Libation Bearers (*Choephoroi*, or *Choephori* in Latin) is the second play in Aeschylus' dramatic entry from 458 BCE, which was called the *Oresteia* ('The Orestes Story').[1] Four plays by the poet were performed on the same day as part of a theatrical competition at the City Dionysia, an annual festival in Athens for the god Dionysus, and three of them have survived to the present day. *Agamemnon* depicted the return of Orestes' father Agamemnon from Troy and his murder by his wife Clytaemestra. In *Libation Bearers*, Orestes returns from exile and exacts revenge against his mother and her lover Aegisthus, but is apparently driven mad by his mother's furies, the supernatural beings of revenge known as the Erinyes. *Eumenides* presents Orestes fleeing to Delphi and then Athens, where the goddess Athena presides and acquits Orestes for his matricide in the first murder trial, as the Erinyes are transformed into Eumenides ('Kindly Ones') and given a cult presence in Athens. The fourth play is lost, and survives only in fragments. *Proteus* was not a tragedy but a satyr play, and likely presented Agamemnon's brother Menelaus in Egypt with his wife Helen. Satyr plays could provide a counterpoint to key themes in a mock-tragic tone that was, it seems, a central part of the experience of tragedy at the Dionysia.

As the 'middle' tragedy of the *Oresteia*, the only extant tragic trilogy to survive from antiquity, *Libation Bearers* creates part of its meaning through juxtaposition with the previous play, *Agamemnon*. Both plays stage the *nostos* (homecoming) of a man to the city of Argos, but while Agamemnon's return had been triumphant, that of his son Orestes is understated. Similarly, the play plants seeds that do not pay off for the audience fully until *Eumenides*. The understanding of divine justice presented in *Libation Bearers* is deliberately incomplete, and the development of this theme in *Eumenides* aggressively and unexpectedly skews towards contemporary Athenian politics. We know virtually nothing about the way *Libation Bearers* resonated with *Proteus*.[2] Yet to understand *Libation Bearers* it is necessary continually to refer to the other two tragedies.

One can even ask if it is proper to treat it as an independent play, separable from the surviving trilogy. I believe it is, and that the play creates its meaning both within itself and in relation to its companion plays. As will be seen with *Persians* (Chapter 1.1), Aeschylus himself could separate a single play from its tetralogy, allowing it to create meaning on its own. Further, as discussed in Chapter 2.4, *Libation Bearers* was seen as separable in this way later in the fifth century. A play makes meaning both as an independent unit and in the larger grouping of plays with which it is performed. Typically with extant Greek tragedy, only the former is available to us today. The *Oresteia* is an exception, allowing us to consider plays both as individual works and as part of a set. The opportunity to consider the set, however, should not remove the option of considering the work as an individual play as well.

The Greater Dionysia (also called the City Dionysia) was an annual festival that celebrated the god Dionysus with processions, sacrifices and artistic competitions.[3] Many festivals contained this competitive element, as individuals strived to distinguish themselves as part of the celebration of the god. Prizes were awarded in different categories, and a successful producer (the *chorēgos*) was able to erect a monument to his victory. Financial backing of the arts was one way that the richest citizens of Athens contributed to civic welfare: liturgies like this were a kind of civic tax that were used to support choral performances (*chorēgia*) or to outfit warships (*trierarcheia*). This pairing points to the crucial importance of choral competition to the Athenian mindset. Festivals were religious events, civic and political events and artistic events – all three of these vectors are constantly operating – and the City Dionysia was the premiere opportunity to showcase drama. All Athenian plays were in verse, with lines that could be spoken (in iambic trimeter), chanted (as with anapests, another metre used) or sung (represented by a wide variety of metrical structures, each of which is unique and constantly shifting). Theatre was publicly performed poetry. Later in the fifth century, more competitions were introduced: *c.* 449 a prize was introduced for the best actor (or set of actors; this could be awarded separately from the best production), and theatrical contests were introduced at other festivals, including the Lenaia and at deme (village) festivals. Prizes were awarded by judges selected from the ten tribes of Athens (the tribal divisions were part of the democratic reforms attributed to Cleisthenes in 508/7). A system was developed that meant not all the votes cast were in fact read: this prevented ties and could be thought to allow the gods to have input into the result (albeit less directly than Athena does at *Eum.* 734–41).[4]

Libation Bearers survives on a thread. The tenth or eleventh century manuscript, the Codex Laurentianus Mediceus 32.9, known as M, once contained all seven extant plays of Aeschylus (though some are damaged), as well as the plays of Sophocles and Apollonius' epic *Argonautica* (for which the manuscript is designated L). While some plays have other manuscript support, the preservation of *Libation Bearers* and *Suppliant Women* (*Hiketides*) here is unique. Though this is the earliest Aeschylean manuscript, much of *Agamemnon*, including its ending, and the opening lines of *Libation Bearers* are missing. The play as preserved in M was copied in the fifteenth century, and occasionally a scribe would introduce corrections on his own initiative.[5] Apart from these two manuscripts the first two thousand years of the play's textual history is almost completely lost to us, and we have no true idea of the extent of the damage that had been done in that time. As if to prove the point, the lines cited by Aristophanes as the start of 'the Orestes story' are not found in the *Oresteia* at all, as is discussed at the beginning of Chapter 2. Scholars assume a page had been lost from the source of M, and that the extant text picks up part way through the prologue. There are no substantial papyrus fragments of the play. As a result, there are many uncertainties throughout the text of the play, and it is risky to hang too much on the interpretation of any given line.

Libation Bearers is an amazing play that is often taken for granted: we know the majestic grandeur of *Agamemnon*, in which the hero's *nostos* provides a context for introducing the amazing character of Clytaemestra; and we recognize the crucial articulation of Athenian cultural values in *Eumenides*, in the origin (*aition*) provided for the Areopagus, and their immediate subversion in light of the reforms to the Areopagus attributed to Ephialtes. Yoking these two is the story of Orestes' matricide. With a moral dilemma that is meaningfully compared to that of Hamlet,[6] the longest and most complex lyric composition in any extant Greek tragedy, and a dizzying fury of stage action that is deliberately disorienting and reflects the inner turmoil Orestes is feeling, *Libation Bearers* is the heart of the *Oresteia*.

1.1 Aeschylus

Aeschylus is the first individual to emerge in the history of the Greek theatre from the shadowy backdrop of legend. Part of that is due to the accident of survival (there were theatrical artists in Athens previous to and contemporary with him), but the survival of these few plays helps us understand the creative mind that produced them. In the first half of the fifth century, there were not many theatrical artists, and it seems Aeschylus was responsible for much of the production himself. He was the playwright, the director (*didaskalos*), the choreographer and, at least in part, the composer of the play's music. During the performance, Aeschylus was also one of the three actors; in 458, the others were (possibly) Cleander and Mynniscus.[7] Because the *Oresteia* in particular proved so enduring, in the fifth century and thereafter, it is fair to say that Aeschylus' individual character has imprinted itself on subsequent theatrical history to an unparalleled degree.

Six (and maybe seven) plays of Aeschylus survive, three of which are from the *Oresteia*, produced in 458. This was near the end of the playwright's life, and may have been his last competitive entry at the Dionysia. Little is known about his life. Ancient biography is often fanciful, and for the early fifth century there is little that is certain. Two sources provide the bulk of the information that we have: an anonymous post-classical biography (the 'Life' or *Vita*) and the *Marmor Parium*, a marble stele from the island of Paros, inscribed *c.* 263, which records a wide range of dates drawn from a

range of sources, some of which are presumably reliable. Additional
details emerge from a variety of sources. It is right to maintain a
considerable degree of skepticism with all of them, since details
from plays are often made biographical. For example, *Vita* 10 claims
that Aeschylus died when a tortoise (from whose shell a lyre might
be made) was dropped on his head by an eagle (the bird of Zeus).
Such an auspicious death seemed to someone as appropriate for the
tragedian whose music was celebrated and whose plays presented
theologically aggressive views; but is it not to be believed.

It seems probable that Aeschylus fought as a soldier at the battle
of Marathon against the invading Persian army in 490 (so *Marm.
Par.* and *Vita* 11, which preserves an epitaph isolating this as
his greatest accomplishment), and perhaps also at Salamis in 480.
Athens was evacuated and occupied by the Persians, who destroyed
the Acropolis. The Persian Wars (an account of which is preserved
in the historian Herodotus) were the first real test of the Athenian
democracy, and Aeschylus was right to be proud of his involvement.
This military experience suggests he was born sometime before
c. 510, but it need not be as early as 525/4 (the date given on *Marm.
Par.*). Suggestions that his first competition was in 499 (from the
Suda, a Byzantine encyclopedia), and his first victory in 484 (*Marm.
Par.*) are possible, but again not certain: all three of these dates seem
conveniently related (first competition at age twenty-five, first victory
at forty). An initial victory in 484 could generate the other dates as
seemingly appropriate, but without historical support. Fortunately,
none of this affects our understanding of Aeschylus' career, since his
extant plays were all produced later.

Aeschylus was born in the village of Eleusis, on the outskirts of
the area controlled by Athens, into an aristocratic family. Eleusis was
the centre of the cult worship of Demeter and Kore – the Eleusinian
Mysteries. Curiously, Aristotle (*Eth. Nic.* 1111a 8–10) records that
Aeschylus at some point was accused of divulging the Mysteries

(possibly within one of his plays). The cult was widely practiced but did contain secrets for initiates only. Whether or not Aeschylus was guilty (Aristotle suggests Aeschylus 'did not know it was a secret'), an accusation of this religious violation is plausible for a playwright presenting politically-engaged theatre. The story appears to have been widely known, as the comic playwright Aristophanes makes a joke about it in 405 (*Frogs* 886–7).

Three extant plays predate the *Oresteia*. The earliest of these is *Persians*, which was produced in 472 in a tetralogy with *Phineus*, *Glaucus of Potniae*, and the satyr play *Prometheus the Fire-Bearer*. *Persians* reflects on the historical battle of Salamis, fought eight years previously, imagining the reaction to events in the Persian court. This is not the only historical tragedy from this period (the tragedian Phrynichus had been fined for his production of *The Capture of Miletus* in 493 or 492), but the subject matter appears significant when it is realized that the ambitious young Pericles was the tetralogy's *chorēgos* (producer).[8] It also shows that not all tetralogies were narratively linked (the other three plays are mythological, though thematic or other correspondences not discernable today may have existed). Success in tragedy represented social capital for all involved, and this was part of how Pericles introduced himself to Athenian politics. *Seven against Thebes* was produced in 467 in a Theban tetralogy that included *Laius*, *Oedipus*, and the satyr-play *Sphinx*. *Suppliant Women* was probably produced in an Egyptian tetralogy, with *Danaids*, *Egyptians*, and the satyr play *Amymone*. A papyrus from the Greek city of Oxyrhynchus in Egypt and published in 1952 (*P. Oxy.* 2256) records a victory result suggesting that the tetralogy was produced between 470 and 459, and a strong case can be made for the year 463.

Many of Aeschylus' dramatic entries (but not all, as the plays of 472 demonstrate) appear to have been constructed with an overarching connecting narrative, as in the *Oresteia*.[9] This is a technique practiced only occasionally by Sophocles and Euripides (though in 415 Euripides composed a Trojan tetralogy which included the extant *Trojan Women*). Much of Aeschylus' work is lost: we have titles and fragments from almost eighty plays altogether (the Suda indicates the total was ninety plays). Numbers like this can seem implausible, but since Dionysia performances involved four plays for each dramatic entry, the number of productions is much lower. Of the surviving titles, seventeen to nineteen are probably satyric. This is what we should expect if his plays were typically presented at the Dionysia: nineteen satyr plays would account for seventy-six of the total number of plays performed in Athens, plus a few anomalies such as performances elsewhere. Of the Dionysia entries, the anonymous biography says Aeschylus came first in the competition thirteen times (*Vita* 13; the Suda says twenty-eight victories, but numbers are easily corrupted in the manuscript tradition). This means Aeschylus won at the Dionysia on average every two years, counting from his initial victory in 484.

Aeschylus was invited to Sicily to stage plays for the tyrant Hieron of Syracuse. Hieron, whose athletic victories (as the owner of racehorses) are commemorated in several extant odes of Pindar and Bacchylides, also wanted to cultivate the Athenian genre of tragedy. A performance of *Persians* in 470 seems likely (independent of its original tetralogy), along with *Women of Aetna*, a new play written for initial performance in Syracuse.[10] Aeschylus returned to Athens, but following the *Oresteia* in 458 he returned to Sicily where he died in the year 456/5, in the town of Gela.

The next generation of his family continued Aeschylus' theatrical tradition. His son Euphorion, named after Aeschylus' father, was victorious at the Dionysia in 431 against the playwrights Sophocles and Euripides. A special license was provided to re-stage Aeschylean plays in the years after his death (*Vita* 12), which will be examined in Chapter 2.4. It is possible, but by no means necessary, that Euphorion won staging plays written by his father. Aeschylus' other son Euaeon was also a playwright, as was his nephew Philocles, whose dramatic entry defeated Sophocles' *Oedipus Tyrannos* and its companion plays in the 420s.[11]

The seventh play to survive among the manuscripts of Aeschylus is *Prometheus Bound*, and scholarly opinion is sharply divided as to its authorship. Though it was assumed to be Aeschylean until the nineteenth century, issues of word choice, metre, and theological stance seem at odds with what is seen in the other extant plays. That may be an accident of survival, and of course a playwright can present different theological views across the body of his work. More significantly, the stage resources required go beyond what seems to have been available in Aeschylus' theatre. The play may date as late as 430; possibly it was presented by Aeschylus' son Euphorion in the 430s with its companion play *Prometheus Unbound*, either as an original play or a rewritten version of his father's play.[12]

1.2 Justice in Athens

The fundamental principle of retributive justice prevalent in Aeschylus' Athens is epitomized in two words: *drasanti pathein*, '[it is necessary] for the one who does [something] to suffer' (*LB* 313). This is typically rendered less formally as 'The doer suffers', and articulates the continued cycle of violence that the *Oresteia* scrutinizes. Clytaemestra kills her husband, and so she must suffer at the hands of Agamemnon's nearest blood-kin, his son Orestes. This act of revenge makes Orestes a 'doer', so that he must, in turn, suffer too. In *Agamemnon*, Zeus provides mortals with the law of 'learning by suffering' (*Ag.* 177 *pathei mathos*); after the sacrifice of Iphigenia, the chorus repeats how Justice, *Dikē*, looms over the Trojans, so that they may 'suffer and learn' (*Ag.* 250 *tois men pathousin mathein*); as long as Zeus is in power, 'the doer suffers' (*Ag.* 1564, *pathein ton erxanta*); Clytemnestra sends the chorus home 'before you suffer for what you have done' (*Ag.* 1658 *prin pathein erxantes*).[13] The cycle of violence, played out in an individual family but equally appropriate for a ten-year war, is what the *Oresteia* seeks to understand. Can human courts, supported by the gods, provide a resolution to this cycle, whereby justice (*dikē*) can be achieved without bloodshed that results in further pollution?

The word *dikē*, a key term in the tetralogy, can embody this sense of 'retribution', but its range of possible meanings extends to include 'revenge', 'punishment', 'penalty', 'case', 'right', and 'justice'. At different points, an Aeschylean usage might demand any of these meanings. It is not that the Greek word means different things: rather, the semantic range of *dikē* and its compounds embodies some aspect of all of these senses. The *Oresteia* is about *dikē*, as it exists among the gods, between gods and humans, as an organizing principle in human society, as an expression of legal practice, and as an ethical principle.[14]

The universe is not fair, however, and it is not always perceptible to humans that wrongdoers do suffer or learn anything. Punishment or recompense may not come for years, or even generations: 'What is fated has waited long' (*LB* 464). The ancestral curse of the house of Atreus (Agamemnon's father) is one cause for the actions depicted in these plays. The crimes of earlier generations (invoking the names Atreus, Thyestes, Pleisthenes and Tanatalus, whose genealogical connection will have been familiar to the audience) are not foregrounded by Aeschylus, but nor are they absent (*Ag.* 1468–84, 1501–2, 1508, 1569, 1583–1602). They continue to have an effect, but they do not themselves cause the crimes of the present, at Troy or elsewhere (*Ag.* 58–71, 367–84), and so new offences also require divine punishment. Strife, an immortal personified force, is always operating (*LB* 474). The presence of Fate and the will of the gods does not absolve individuals of personal responsibility: humans make choices, and the cosmic cycles of justice are only one explanation of the evil that men and women do. The reasons that people provide for their actions are not complete explanations for their behaviour.

The world of Aeschylean tragedy, as with the world of Homer's *Iliad*, is one in which humans make choices that have been fated long before, but this in no way absolves them of the moral consequences of their actions. It is not a playwright's job to resolve theological questions surrounding free will. What he can do, however, is dramatize a situation in which a freely chosen action that is unambiguously good – the rightful revenge of a murdered father – is at the same time one of the most horrific, monstrous crimes imaginable – the murder of one's own mother. Neither Orestes nor Clytaemestra gains any special insight over the course of the play. Their situation is presented instead to help the audience grapple with the profound, immoral, confusing realities recognized by those living in fifth-century Athens.

A number of related political events inform the circumstances of the *Oresteia*. Athens made a peace treaty with the *polis* of Argos *c.* 462 (Thuc. 1.102.4), shifting its political support towards this city and away from Sparta. It is hard to believe that Aeschylus' decision to make Argos Agamemnon's capital rather than Mycenae is not related in some way to this alliance and to this significant shift in Athenian foreign policy. Further, a series of democratic political reforms were initiated by Ephialtes, an ally of the younger Pericles. The Areopagus ('the Hill of Ares') was the senior lawcourt at Athens, which was composed of former archons. Due to Ephialtes' reforms, its powers had been significantly reduced by 462: the Areopagus was the court for murder trials and certain religious crimes (such as the removing of olive trees; cf. Lysias 7), but it was no longer the political force that it had been following the ostracism of Themistocles to Argos in 472/1. This is one end of a process that had begun with the democratic reforms of Cleisthenes almost fifty years earlier. For some, this change merely returned the Areopagus to its original function; for others it limited the power of the court, redistributing it to other venues, including the *dikastēria*, the jury courts of Athens.[15] Aeschylus of course does not spell out his relationship to these reforms, and different spectators will understand the relationship of the *Oresteia* to them differently – as indeed do modern critics. I see Aeschylus supporting democratic reform, but recognizing that courts can and do produce flawed results; human *dikē* is imperfect but it is nevertheless worth pursuing. Other cogent interpretations are possible. Again it is hard not to connect this recent political change in Athens with the events depicted in *Eumenides*, in which Orestes is tried for murder at the Areopagus, providing a mythic origin (*aition*) for this function of the court. Ephialtes was assassinated (the first known political assassination in Greece), and in the 420s the culprit had not been identified (Antiphon 5.68). One individual is later associated with the killing, Aristodikos of Tanagra, who may even have fled Attica after the event, but crucially no one was ever tried for the killing.[16] Aeschylus' use of Argos and the Areopagus was not innocuous to the eyes of an informed Athenian citizen in 458.

Eumenides presents a trial in which the legal procedure seems dodgy, and the result, a split decision which exonerates Orestes, is open to critique on a number of fronts. Admittedly, this polyvalence is not always articulated or presented, but insistence on a single linear interpretation limits discussions and makes Aeschylus seem more primal than he is. *Eumenides* does not offer an idealized origin story for the court-system, and any spectator would be right to consider whether Athena's actions in the play produce a dramatically satisfying or theologically tolerable result. It is not obvious that they do. Aeschylus does not sacrifice theatrical effectiveness to make a specific political point. Instead he creates a drama where meaning is not clear, and the direct intervention of the gods in human affairs does not produce an unambiguously positive result. If it is true that '*Eumenides* transforms the tragic inevitabilities of *Agamemnon* and

Libation Bearers into confident hope,[17] that transformation comes at a cost that is reflected in the imperfect judgements and apparent injustices evident in everyday life. This is intellectually challenging, and helps make the tetralogy so profound.[18]

The resolution that Aeschylus provides does not claim that the gods are necessarily just, and a suspicion about theodicy underlies much of what precedes: Agamemnon's death may be a divine punishment, but it is equally motivated by the base designs of Clytaemestra; Orestes follows divine instructions into committing what is objectively a horrific and amoral act, and is punished for doing so. Agamemnon, Clytaemestra, and Orestes all have personal motivations for what they do, and at the same time each is an agent of the gods. Do the courts, as human embodiments of societal will for justice, achieve their ends? Do they do so legitimately, and with divine sanction? The Areopagus appears at its foundation as a broken institution, but it is one that provides a human, social solution for the intractable problems of evil. While *Eumenides* provides an answer to the ethical problem presented in *Libation Bearers*, it does so only through compromise (offering new honours and a new Athenian name to the Erinyes) and deflection (that Apollo ordered the killing does not absolve Orestes from committing it) and equivocation (as both Apollo and Athena pursue their personal agendas without regard for Zeus' ethical absolutes). The moral complexity and richness of the *Oresteia* emerges because there is no certain answer to the questions posed. There is only the problem, and a recognition that human institutions struggle with it.

While it is possible to interpret the *Oresteia* as providing a linear development from some 'primitive' sense of right to the well-ordered good governance of a democratic *polis*, Aeschylus consistently challenges this evolutionary view. *Dikē* is in conflict with *dikē* (*LB* 461). Prescribed gender roles in Athens further complicate any clean message, as Athena's dubious rationale for favoring Orestes

(*Eum.* 734–43) resonates uncomfortably in the light of Clytaemestra's legitimate challenge to masculine authority (as represented by Agamemnon and Zeus). Clytaemestra and Athena are counterpoints to each other, both androgynous, human and divine in opposition, and in *Eumenides* are played by the same actor.

The smooth running of the *polis* represents another crucial theme of the *Oresteia*. Aeschylus was born before the democratic reforms of Cleisthenes in 508/7, and he had survived the sack of Athens by the Persians in 480. The threat of foreign invasion and tyranny are found throughout his work. The performance of *Persians* in 472 is interwoven both with the democratic politician Pericles and (in its performance soon thereafter) with the Sicilian tyrant Hieron, and the play makes its meaning differently in those two contexts. In *Libation Bearers*, Orestes stands over the bodies of Clytaemestra and Aegisthus decrying the 'twin tyrants of this land' (*LB* 973), but it is too simplistic to read this moment as a symbol of democratic reform. These tensions persist. In the 440s, following Aeschylus' death, Pericles would build the Odeion, a large, square, roofed building evocative of a Persian tent, on an area partially overlapping with the precinct of the Theatre of Dionysus in Athens. Among its other functions, the Odeion was the site of singing competitions and of some preliminary activities at the City Dionysia. The democratic victory over foreign tyranny was thereby celebrated in a space associated with the theatre and performance.

1.3 The Theatre of Dionysus

The year 458 or soon before also marked a time of significant innovation in the use of the theatre space, and the *Oresteia* is the earliest witness to these changes. Earlier surviving Aeschylean plays all presume similar performance conditions, with the audience seated around much of an open dancing space, the *orchēstra*. The *orchēstra* of the Theatre of Dionysus is on the southeast slope of the Acropolis, and was *c*. 25 metres in diameter. Near its centre was an altar, the *thymelē*.[19] This was the notional focus of the *orchēstra* and was probably the same altar used during pre-play ceremonies to honour the god Dionysus. We cannot say how large or elaborate the *thymelē* was, but it provided a focus around which the chorus could dance, and it could be identified as a specific location in a play. Audiences of maybe 7,000–10,000 individuals, citizens and non-citizens, predominantly male but likely with some women there as well, were seated in the *theatron* on wooden benches that were placed on the hillside slope, with the majority of spectators looking down onto the dancing space. Characters could enter from stage left or stage right, and interact with the chorus. In the large, open-air space, the arrival of a character was processional, and could be accompanied by music or song.

It is seldom helpful to guess about the 'origins' of theatre in Athens, but correspondences with other forms of choral dance that pre-existed Aeschylus, particularly the dithyramb in which choruses of fifty men or boys would also compete, emphasize the crucial importance of the chorus as a unified dramatic character and provide a model for theatrical dialogue as individual speakers engage with a collective group. At the Dionysia, each of ten tribes (one of the levels of political organization in democratic Athens) would field two dithyrambic choruses, which meant that there would be 1,000 choral dancers at this festival alone (in addition to those performing in tragic and comic choruses), each of whom would be alert to the nuances of music and choreography and the technical demands of sung performance. The audience was literate in the vocabulary of music and dance.

Athenians often generated evolutionary models, one of which ascribed the innovation of 'theatre' (i.e. one actor interacting with a chorus) to Thespis at some point in the later sixth century, two actors with a chorus to Aeschylus, and three actors with a chorus to Sophocles (Aristotle, *Poetics* 1449a 18). Theatre was a space for innovation, for developing new and exciting ways of presenting narratives. The *Oresteia* in 458 represents the earliest certain point when three actors were in place. It is also the first certain use of the *skēnē*, a wooden building that served as a backdrop to the *orchēstra*. Both of these features, if not completely new, were innovations of the previous decade. Both require deeper consideration to understand how Athenian theatre operated. As it turns out, *Libation Bearers* represents the greatest challenge to an otherwise consistent understanding of each of them.

The so-called Rule of Three Actors likely emerged as a factor of the competitive environment at the Dionysia. Each playwright, who typically also served as the director (*didaskalos*) of his plays and at this early stage in the development of the theatre was also one of the actors, was assigned notionally equal resources to create a level playing-field for competition. Audiences could therefore reward innovative and the creative use of actors within a play or across a tetralogy. The *Oresteia* is our clearest indication of the sophisticated use to which the Rule could be put. For example, in *Agamemnon*, the same actor probably plays the Watchman, the Herald, Agamemnon, and Aegisthus. This would mean that all the individual men in the play were united, sharing certain vocal and physiological qualities. I believe this actor also plays Orestes in *Libation Bearers* and *Eumenides*, creating an implicit resonance between father and son. This is not the only possible role assignment, but using it also allows for a theatrical 'surprise', as the newly-introduced third actor speaks unexpectedly as Cassandra after standing silent and motionless onstage for hundreds of lines (*Ag.* 783–1072). This actor would also play Pylades in *Libation Bearers* and the Pythia and Apollo in *Eumenides*, providing a unified Apollonine voice for these characters. Another continuity can be effected by having the same actor play Clytaemestra through all three tragedies, and then Athena (apparently two powerfully contrasting roles, which nevertheless share an unfeminine quality). Such doublings do not need to be heavy-handed, and they do not even need to be noticed by every spectator. Yet for those in the audience alert to the shared roles, there is additional information available for interpreting the plays.[20]

In *Libation Bearers*, there are three role assignments that can be discussed now that show some of the ways the play pushed the limits of staging (discussion of a final disposition of actors is postponed until Chapter 3.5). First, the short scene that features Aegisthus (838–54) almost certainly requires the Orestes actor to play Aegisthus as he had in *Agamemnon*. The appearance of Aegisthus is humorous in its brevity, and in Aegisthus' inability to hide his delight at the news of Orestes' supposed death (creating a knowing irony for spectators alert to the role doubling). If we assume consistent casting between the plays of the tetralogy, then Aegisthus leaves the stage at 854, shouts from behind the *skēnē* when he is being killed at 869 and appears as Orestes at 892. This scene is followed almost immediately by the quick appearance of an unnamed slave (875–91, assuming he leaves in response to Clytaemestra's command). Since Orestes and Clytaemestra are onstage together with the slave and again later when Orestes addresses Pylades (899), it follows that this actor must play both the slave and Pylades, and further that he should change costume and mask in this very brief interval. The scholia (marginal comments and interpretations of the text that survive from antiquity) at line 899 writes, 'The messenger-from-within [*exangelos*] changes his costume into Pylades, so that four do not speak'. Similarly, it is no great challenge for the Clytaemestra actor (who appears at 668) also to deliver the Doorkeeper's line at 657 (the Doorkeeper may not even appear onstage, but could remain a voice behind a closed door). Even in this early use of three actors, there is a theatrical virtue in creating the illusion of more performers through the clever employment of doubling.

Nevertheless, for some scholars this change from Servant to Pylades happens too quickly to be a necessary component of the play's stagecraft. It is a quick change, but performed successfully it offers a remarkable *coup de théâtre*, and it has the great potential momentarily to disorient the audience, which has no reason to expect Pylades to speak. His words fix Orestes' determination, and the use of three actors immediately before the critical juncture of the play is part of the theatrical effect. The alternative, if the quick change was not adopted, would require the use of a fourth actor in a tiny role (twelve spoken lines, or three for Pylades), which would apparently be an exception for fifth-century theatre.

The second uncertainty concerns the *skēnē*. The *skēnē* was a temporary one-storey wooden building that was newly erected for each festival and provided a backdrop for the actors. It was painted to represent a generic palace or temple, the precise nature of which would often be made clear by the opening speakers in a play.[21] In *Agamemnon* and *Libation Bearers*, the *skēnē* represents the royal palace of Argos. In the centre of the *skēnē* was a double door. No fifth-century play requires more than a single *skēnē* doorway, if it is allowed that the same door can represent multiple locations over the course of a play.[22] I believe there was only one doorway, but (as we shall see) *Libation Bearers* offers the greatest challenge to that claim.

Apart from *Libation Bearers*, no extant tragedy requires more than a single doorway in the *skēnē*, and (despite arguments of Dover that favour a completely naturalistic representation of stage space[23]) no extant comedy does either. If *Libation Bearers* did employ more than one door, it would either be a resource that remains underutilized for the remainder of the century as far as we can tell, or an experiment that was not preserved in subsequent festivals (for which plays survive). Either of these would be possible, but neither can be proved.[24] This issue will impact the decision of the staging of *LB* 875–99, which is probably the busiest two minutes in extant Greek tragedy (see Chapter 4.4).

The playing space available in the Theatre of Dionysus in Athens therefore consisted of the *orchēstra*, the area immediately before the *skēnē* and the *skēnē* roof.[25] The three speaking actors and unspeaking attendants could occupy any of these locations. The same *skēnē* (with however many doors) would have been used by all competitors, and would have been constructed as part of the general festival preparations and not for the needs of a single dramatic entry. While not required for the staging of any extant scene, visual evidence from vase-painting seems to corroborate the existence of a low (1 metre) wooden platform (*proskēnion*) physically connected to the *skēnē* building and accessed from the *orchēstra* by a few steps.[26] The existence of a demarcated space immediately before the *skēnē* allows for two distinct areas to be used in dynamic tension, clarifying the symbolic distance between the two locations of the performance space, and it arguably provides a firmer surface for the *ekkyklēma*. The *ekkyklēma* (roll-out device) was a wheeled platform that could reveal an interior scene, as happens in this play (*LB* 973, see Chapter 4.7). The *mēchanē* (theatrical crane) was not part of the theatrical resources available in 458.

To call this platform a 'stage' though is mistaken: both platform and *orchēstra* are part of the actors' performance area, and speaking actors will regularly have occupied the dance floor.[27] The altar of Dionysus in the *orchēstra*, the *thymelē*, could represent an altar or tomb within the dramatic setting of the play: this block would become the tomb of Agamemnon in Aeschylus' *Libation Bearers* or the altar of Zeus in Euripides' *Children of Heracles*.[28] There is no indication that the altar's sacred character prevented it assuming a dramatic function, and using this permanent feature seems preferable to erecting a temporary altar near this same location when required for a given play.[29] Some plays may not define the location as meaningful (it is not identified in *Agamemnon*, for example), but it remains available for any play choosing to designate it. Stage properties could be placed on or near it to help define its dramatic function. Fourth-century vase-paintings showing Electra meeting Orestes at the tomb depict vases and sacred fillets on the altar (see Chapter 2.2), and the consistency between these images likely reflects an established practice in the subsequent performance tradition of Aeschylus' play.[30]

The Greek theatre therefore presents the audience with two fundamental axes.[31] The first axis, running roughly north–south, cuts through the *orchēstra* in a line that connects the *thymelē* to the central door of the *skēnē*, continuing inside. The architecture of the space particularly favours a performer standing at or near the *thymelē*, or at or near the door (giving a 'strength' to the location comparable to standing downstage centre in a modern proscenium-arch theatre). The door therefore represents a liminal space, marking a boundary between outside and inside, seen and unseen, tangible and implied. Thresholds carry significance: they mark transitions, and in *Agamemnon* and *Libation Bearers*, it signals (among other things) the transition from life to death. The door also keeps things out of sight, leaving terrors to the more vicious predations of the imagination. The door is an invention, and previously Aeschylus has written for a 'pre-door' tragic theatre: the door's availability changes the rhythm of a play, allowing more sudden, less processional entries. It also asks us to consider what lies beyond the door: it is not simply backstage, where actors change costumes and props are stored. The door leads to an extension of the dramatic world, one not seen by spectators. From the audience perspective, beyond the door to the palace is still Argos, and the description of people and spaces there, the use of voices and offstage sounds all reinforce that dramatic reality. A similar extension of the theatrical world exists along the second axis, which in Athens runs roughly east–west. Offstage locations extend the dramatic world beyond the two *eisodoi*, offering other places to the imagination where action can occur.

Understanding the practical concerns of stage resources and considering the possibilities available to a production are important for modern readers because it is through performance that the play created its meaning. Stage directions were not part of ancient theatre scripts. Even character notations were used infrequently, and exactly who is speaking cannot always be determined from the text. Further, many conventions were different from most modern experiences of theatre. All actors wore helmet-like masks that covered the entire head. Performances occurred during the day, with no artificial lighting. As we will see, the action of *Libation Bearers* is set partly at night, and that stands in tension with the visibility shown to the audience. The year of the *Oresteia* was a time of extensive theatrical innovation, with Aeschylus using the theatre's physical resources as best he was able in order to communicate the plays' themes.

1.4 Myth and Religion

The story of Orestes' revenge was a traditional one, and was presumed knowledge for the audience of Homer's *Odyssey* in the eighth century.[32] Though *Libation Bearers* is the earliest extant continuous narrative of the matricide, the story was by Aeschylus' time familiar in art and literature. Homer had presented Agamemnon (*Od.* 11.435–9) and Cassandra (*Od.* 11. 421–3) as a victim of the guile of Clytaemestra, who had not even closed the king's eyes when he died (*Od.* 11.424–6). The principal engineer of Agamemnon's destruction in Homer had been Aegisthus. This, at least, is Agamemnon's perspective as he speaks to Odysseus from the Underworld. Aegisthus, not Clytaemestra, had set the watch for Agamemnon's return (*Od.* 4.524–9), and Aegisthus had murdered Agamemnon at a banquet (*Od.* 1.300, 4.525–33, 11.410). Both Aegisthus and Clytaemestra are guilty (*Od.* 3.234–5). As an exemplum for Homer's purposes, there is both similarity and contrast between Agamemnon's fate and that of Odysseus. Agamemnon's early, unhappy *nostos* contrasts with Odysseus' late but eventually happy one; Agamemnon had returned openly, and advises Odysseus to arrive in secret; Clytaemestra's infidelity contrasts with Penelope's perseverance against her suitors. Indeed, so fitting are the parallels that it is clear the poet has tailored his presentation of Agamemnon's death to the Odyssean context, and it is not possible to discern what elements are new to the epic description. What is not inverted, however, is the correspondence between Orestes and Telemachus.

Orestes returns from exile in Athens (*Od.* 3.306–8). This detail possibly anticipates the radical surprise of an Athenian location for much of *Eumenides*. Odysseus' son is consistently enjoined to emulate the righteous behaviour of Orestes: i.e. to avenge his father's honour in retribution against his mother's suitors (*Od.* 1.298–302, 3.193–200, 11.448–53). Orestes kills Aegisthus (*Od.* 1.40–3), and, since Menelaus returns from Egypt on the same day Orestes is holding a funeral for Aegisthus and his 'hateful mother' (*Od.* 3.306–12), it may be assumed the audience knows him also as a matricide, even if the poem does not present it as an ethical problem. Heroic young men avenge wronged fathers, and that restores order to a royal house. With the *Oresteia*, this will change: 'After Aeschylus, no one ever again says, "Be like Orestes!" (the famous matricide)'.[33]

The story of Orestes continued to be told in the centuries between the textualization of the *Odyssey* (*c.* 700?) and Aeschylus (458).[34] In the seventh century, Hesiod's *Catalogue of Women* (*Ehoiai* fr. 23a.30 M–W) has Orestes killing his mother. The same source lists Agamemnon's daughters as Electra and Iphimede. Homer, *Iliad* 9.142–5 (= 284–7) had listed Agamemnon's daughters as Chrysothemis, Laodice, and Iphianassa, and we need to go to Aelian, *VH* 4.26 in the second century CE, to be told that a shadowy poet named Xanthus equated Homer's Laodice with Hesiod's Electra, saying she was renamed because she remained *a-lektros*, 'without a wedding bed'. Xanthus was also a source for Stesichorus (Athenaeus 513A; this is all that is known about Xanthus).

An epic poem by Agias of Troezen called *Nostoi* (*Homecomings*), the last of the so-called Epic Cycle, was composed in the sixth century.[35] In the last of its five books, following the murder of Agamemnon by Aegisthus and Clytaemestra, Orestes and Pylades achieve revenge. This is the first mention of Orestes' companion Pylades, the son of Stropheus. Garvie argues for a traditional connection between Pylades the human companion and Hermes as a divine one:[36] Stropheus and Pylaios (and their cognates) are cult titles of Hermes. As at *Odyssey* 3.306–12, *Nostoi* presented Menelaus returning from Troy by way of Egypt immediately following these events. This sequence, then, seems fixed, and is likely to have suggested to Aeschylus the subject of his satyr play in 458, *Proteus*.

The lyric poet Stesichorus (writing in the mid-sixth century) apparently composed an *Oresteia* in two books.[37] The poem is set in Sparta (fr. 216), which at this time was appropriating the Mycenaean heritage (as it was understood) from Argos. Aeschylus' Argive setting a century later can be seen as a corrective to this poetic choice. Among much that could be said about this poem (including its title), a few details relate to *Libation Bearers* specifically. First, there is mention of a lock of hair dedicated by Orestes in a recognition scene; following the matricide, Clytaemestra's Erinyes pursue Orestes, and Apollo gives him a bow to defend himself (fr. 217). Clytaemestra has a foreboding dream (fr. 219), which will be discussed in Chapter 3.2.[38] Finally, Orestes' nurse appears, named Laodamia (fr. 218).[39]

These details are corroborated in the fifth-century by Pindar's epinician ode commissioned for the Theban boy Thrasydaios's victory at Delphi, *Pythian* 11. Orestes returns from Strophius and Pylades to kill Aegisthus and Clytaemestra (*Pyth.* 11.15–16, 34–7), and the poem mentions his nurse, here called Arsinoë (*Pyth.* 11.17–18). The date of *Pythian* 11 is unknown: the victory occurred either in 474 or 454, and so Pindar either predates *Libation Bearers* or immediately succeeds it.[40] There is no certain relationship between Aeschylus and Pindar, and both could depend on a shared knowledge of earlier works.

The visual arts also show an awareness of the story before Aeschylus.[41] Not all can be identified with certainty: is a woman holding an axe necessarily Clytaemestra? That is a question raised by a metope at the Temple of Hera at Foce de Sele (Paestum), where an axe-wielding woman is being restrained by another woman (Electra? the nurse?). Similarly, bronze reliefs from Olympia bear possible but uncertain witness to the story in the sixth century, but again identification is not certain. Better is a terracotta relief perhaps from Melos and now in the Louvre[42] that may predate the play, which shows Electra and another woman (the Nurse?) meeting Orestes and two men (Pylades and Hermes?) at a tomb.[43] Interpretation of these scenes and others is tempting in light of *Libation Bearers*, but over-identification (and consequently mis-identification) is always possible. Possibly, a given image was inspired by Stesichorus, but such speculation cannot be proved. More telling is a splendid kalyx crater by Dokimasia painter,[44] dated *c.* 470, which shows the death of Agamemnon, wrapped in a net, on one side, and the death of Aegisthus on the other. This pairing points to the sequence in *Agamemnon* and *Libation Bearers*, and demonstrates that the net imagery in *Agamemnon* also had its precursors.

What this means is summarized by Gantz: 'The narrative line of the *Choephoroi*, whatever the source of individual details, likely follows in its general shape the run of the story familiar to most Athenians by the time of Aischylos'.[45] Where Aeschylus' greatest innovations emerge, then, is in the moral depth and theological dimension given to Orestes' act, for which there is no resolution. Human institutions such as court trials for murder cannot fully reckon with the issue of revenge. The prominence given to Clytaemestra throughout the tetralogy (with the consequent diminishment of Aegisthus) is a direct result of Aeschylus' desire to magnify the horror of Orestes' choice.

The theological dimension is crucial, for the gods are real and they interfere in the world. Apollo is not opposed to the supernatural forces thought to reside underground (the chthonic world, that 'of the earth'), though he will be opposed to Clytaemestra's Erinyes specifically. The binary is not straightforward, and is deliberately askew, emphasizing a gendered bias. Prayer and sacrifice can grapple with this involvement only imperfectly. The Olympians – Zeus above all, but Hermes, Apollo and eventually Athena are all important for *Libation Bearers* – support Orestes in his revenge. Chthonic forces (darker supernatural forces including the Erinyes and the spirits of the dead) are seen to pre-exist Olympian sovereignty, but also make their wills known. The confluence of Olympian and chthonic forces run parallel to Orestes' human decision: '*Choephori* is marked by a convergence of powers all driving Orestes towards the same act'.[46] Zeus wills it (*LB* 244–6, 306, 639–45, 783–8, 948–52, supported by Apollo 269–97, 900–2, 953–6, 1029–33); Agamemnon demands it (*LB* 1–9, 124–51, 479–80, 925); and Orestes chooses it (*LB* 298–305, 1029–32). The operational coexistence of these motivations is central to the religious dimension of the play.

Religion and festival culture were deeply engrained in Athenian civic and family life: the gods and a range of supernatural forces, including chthonic ones as just discussed, shape and impact everyday realities. This creates a dense network of associations that would be intimately felt by the spectators in the Theatre of Dionysus, but which we can only partially grasp today. Consider, for example, the Anthesteria, a three-day Athenian festival held just over a month before the Dionysia.[47] This also was a festival to Dionysus, and each of the three days was associated with a different kind of vessel. The first day, Pithoigia, celebrated the opening of the large jars (*pithoi*) of the last year's wine. The second day, Choes, involved the pouring of wine from pitchers (*choes*) in a day that featured a drinking contest led by the archon basileus, the chief magistrate in Classical Athens who also had responsibilities for the City Dionysia. Drinking was announced by a trumpet call: 'The ritual was based upon that which, according to tradition, had been observed when Orestes was entertained in Athens before he had been purified of murder; to avoid pollution each drinker had a separate vessel, and all drank in silence'.[48] The day concluded with the offering of libations to the dead. The third day, Chrytoi, continued the offerings for the dead with the manufacture of a grain porridge in pots (*chrytoi*) offered to Hermes Chthonios.

The correspondence between these elements of the Anthesteria and *Libation Bearers* is striking. The prominence of Hermes Chthonios, the appeasement of dead relatives, and the prominent use of the *chous* in the second of three stages of the celebration, with the specific connection to the Athenian purification of Orestes, does suggest that there are specific correspondences that would be identified by any Athenian citizen in the audience. These associations deepen the meaning of the first half of *Libation Bearers* in ways that do not need to be outlined precisely for us to recognize the festival's importance to interpreting the *Oresteia*. Aeschylus is using a ritual pattern to make the initial action of his play somewhat more familiar to his audience. Further, there are indications that it was at the Anthesteria that actors were selected for the Dionysia.[49] This in turn offers the clearest indication that we have of the length of rehearsal periods for the Dionysia. The Anthesteria was a festival of Dionysus that pointed towards the coming Dionysia, for which specific associations with the plot and themes of the *Oresteia* and Orestes' specific need for purification already existed in Athens.

Reperformance and Recognition

'First, tell me the prologue of the *Oresteia*' (Aristophanes, *Frogs* 1124): in Aristophanes' comedy from 405 the dead playwright Aeschylus, a character in the play, is told to recite the opening lines from his plays of 458. This is the earliest explicit mention of Aeschylus' tetralogy, and the line is revealing for two reasons. First, as the jokes that follow in *Frogs* 1125–76 demonstrate, the verses recited by Aeschylus are not in the manuscripts for the *Oresteia*. From this and other sources, there are five surviving fragments, which provide all or parts of eleven lines of what has been lost before the manuscript version of the prologue begins, from a total of at most thirty lines.[1] It is only because of this passage, emphasizing the importance of the plays of 458, that we even know how 'the *Oresteia*' started. Second, the lines themselves are only appropriate as the prologue to *Libation Bearers*: Orestes returning to his native country approaches the grave of his murdered father, Agamemnon. While the nature of play titles in Athens is not entirely problem-free,[2] it is not the case that '*Oresteia*' refers to *Libation Bearers* only. The *–eia* ending (used in the Greek for titles of epics such as the *Odyssey* and for other tetralogies) is not used elsewhere for a single play. In what sense, then, is *Libation Bearers* a beginning? The answer to this question is different for a modern reader than for an ancient spectator, but asking it encourages consideration of the *anagnōrisis* (recognition) scene between the Orestes and Electra, and examination of the reception of *Libation Bearers* in the first century of the play's existence.

Agamemnon had ended with Clytaemestra victorious: having accomplished the plan that she had intended long before Agamemnon returned home, she stands over his body and that of Cassandra, still in power and unthreatened by any avenger, even if one had been predicted by Cassandra (*Ag.* 1280–3). Orestes, her son, has been sent away (*Ag.* 877–86) and seven years later (in the eighth year) he returns (Aeschylus seems to inherit this detail from *Od.* 3.306–9). Orestes, an infant when Agamemnon sailed to Troy, is therefore returning at the cusp of adulthood, and his return is to be seen as his first act as a grown man.

The original audience may have had no idea what the content of *Libation Bearers* was to be. The play's title provides no interpretable clues, even assuming that the title was somehow made available in advance, as happened later in the century at the preliminary ceremony known as the Proagon.[3] Would spectators expect the *skēnē* to represent the same location in the second play as in the first? We know of no other plays where that continuity of space is maintained (it is unlikely to emerge in a tetralogy not narratively linked). The setting for *Libation Bearers* – same place, years later – might therefore be thought of as unique. In any case, at the start of the play the stage would look like that of *Agamemnon*: unadorned and undifferentiated.

2.1 Offerings at a Tomb

As in *Agamemnon*, *Libation Bearers* begins with a descendant of Atreus coming home. In this case, it's the grandson, and the *nostos* is different than the grand entry of his father seen in the previous play. Orestes and Pylades (named in line 20) enter along an *eisodos*, and head to the altar in the centre of the *orchēstra*. Agamemnon had entered in a chariot with a procession, and with a train of captured treasures, declaring his victory. Here, the two young men approach on foot, alone, carrying their own baggage (*LB* 675). They are dressed as travellers, likely each wearing a broad-brimmed hat (*petasos*). This is the hat often seen on images of the god Hermes, signalling him as a messenger. Within the dramatic world, they approach the tomb of Agamemnon, which is at the centre of the *orchēstra*.

I believe that the *thymelē* serves as the tomb of Agamemnon, establishing the motivation for Orestes' action at the focal centre of each spectator's visual field.[4] It is possible that between *Agamemnon* and *Libation Bearers* there was some visual change to whatever was there to mark the burial, but ultimately that is not needed: the words of the text (*LB* 4) are sufficient to define the location unambiguously. Later plays, particularly Euripides' *Helen* (797–801) and Aristophanes' *Thesmophoriazusae* (881–91), make explicit the practice of using an altar to represent a tomb in the dramatic world. Indeed, the substitution seems to be reflected when the chorus says it is 'respecting your father's tomb as an altar ...' (*LB* 106).[5] Other staging solutions are possible, but less probable. Whatever happened on stage, it is important that the playwright creates a visual echo between the two homecomings, inviting spectators when they see Orestes to read his *nostos* against that of Agamemnon. Parallel stage-craft within the tetralogy adds depth to the meaning of the event, allowing spectators to perceive something that is beyond the under-standing of the characters themselves. This technique, which Taplin calls 'mirror scenes',[6] is used more widely in this play than Taplin describes, and the parallelism in this case is important. Agamemnon's chariot stopped somewhere in the *orchēstra*, and it is at that point that this play represents his tomb and invites, I believe, the audience to perceive the resonances between father and son.

The play begins with Orestes speaking, 'Chthonian Hermes, overseer of a father's authority, become, I beseech you, my saviour and my ally' (*LB* 1–2). Possibly his sword is drawn in caution.[7] Orestes' opening invocation of Hermes is appropriate for a number of reasons. Explicitly, in his chthonian aspect he is a god of the Underworld, ferrying souls of the dead to the world below. He has access to Agamemnon's ghost. The chthonic aspect recognizes a tension between the Olympian gods and those beneath the earth, and supernatural forces from both places will drive the action of the play. Hermes is both a god of travellers, appropriately invoked after a long journey, and a god of duplicity, fitting for the secret homecoming that Orestes is undertaking. Hermes is also a son of a powerful father, as is Orestes: an ambiguity exists in line 1, where it is unclear whether Zeus' authority or that of Agamemnon is meant. It does not follow, however, that there is a visible statue of Hermes in the performance area, as has sometimes been suggested.[8] Orestes' piety is foregrounded in this speech, and the silent presence of Pylades, who will himself prove to be both an ally and a saviour, creates the impression that Orestes is not acting alone.[9] Pylades' silence is a dramatic choice: Aeschylus could have had three actors speaking throughout the play's first half, and the decision to keep Pylades silent provides a powerful surprise when he does eventually speak (900–2).

Orestes offers a lock of his hair, an appropriate gift both in memory of his father and to Inachus, who is both the ancestral king of Argos and another non-Olympian divinity, the river-god of the Inachus river (*LB* 6–7). The offering to Inachus has already taken place, but the audience sees the gift to Agamemnon. Possibly a detachable lock is affixed to the Orestes mask, and the actor mimes removing it, cutting it with his sword; or perhaps the offering itself is mimed, since a lock would be a small stage property in any case in the large Athenian outdoor performance space.

This ritual activity is interrupted, as the chorus of palace slaves emerges from the *skēnē*, holding vases filled with liquid offerings also destined for Agamemnon's tomb. Again, the stagecraft is uncertain, but if the tomb is situated in the *orchēstra,* Scullion is correct that the best visual sense is created if the chorus emerges from the stage building, which will be defined as the palace in the second half of the play.[10] Orestes identifies them and their purpose instantly: they are *choas pherousas,* 'bearing libations' (*LB* 15). They are dressed in torn black clothes of mourning (11, 28–9), their masks perhaps marked with gashed cheeks (25), and behind them follows Electra (16–18). The dozen women of the chorus appear as mourners, and it will soon emerge that the death they are mourning is that of Agamemnon as well. This striking coincidence is one way the play shows Zeus' engineering of events, but dramaturgically it also compresses the time since the end of the last play. Argos has held its breath for seven years, it seems, and only now is its former king being laid to rest in a ritually acceptable manner.

The libation bearers in *Libation Bearers* enter bearing libations. This detail is easily overlooked, but it is important and needs to be argued.[11] Published translations can overlook stage props in the *Oresteia,* and in this case there is some degree of freedom allowed by the page that cannot remain undecided in production. Liquid offerings are brought to the tomb, somehow. Sommerstein is aware of the issue, and his stage direction suggests two members of the chorus 'carry jars on their heads'; a few lines later Electra 'comes out of the door, a little after the others, also carrying a jar'.[12] By restricting the number of choristers with offerings to two, Sommerstein points to another issue. There are three possible answers to how many choristers carry libations: none, some or all. Line 15 shows that the answer is not none. Sommerstein opts for some. If two choristers carry something, or one, or three or six, libations are brought on stage and there is something to be poured. I can see no reason why the answer could not be that all choristers are carrying grave offerings, however, and that instead of trying to minimize the issue of stage props, their presence was emphasized. When an elderly male chorus makes reference to walking sticks (*Ag.* 75), there is no corresponding impulse to suggest that only the *koryphaios* (the chorus leader) has a walking stick, or that only some of the group do. Scholars never-theless have shied away from the amount of libations (why? because they are messy?), even though the only internal motivation for the slave women's arrival is that they have been sent by a conscience-stricken Clytaemestra to bring offerings to Agamemnon's grave.

Liquid offerings would typically be of wine, honey, or water, and the fluids would naturally belong in a variety of containers. Single-handled *oinochoai* (wine-jugs) would obviously be the expected shape (the entry song regularly refers to pouring and to *choes*, and the shape is particularly associated with the dead through their promi-nence in day two of the Anthesteria), but some choristers might be carrying other vessels, such as *hydriae* (water-jugs). Athenian fifth-century vase-painting regularly shows scenes of libations being poured, by men and women, in a variety of ritual contexts. By giving the chorus props that are carried asymmetrically (either in one hand or on one shoulder), Aeschylus instantly creates a situation in which the choreography of the servile chorus is visually distinctive. The entrance song, or *parodos*, was a theatrical highlight, providing the first opportunity for the audience to observe the chorus' collective character. Similarly, Aeschylus' lost play *Semele* had an alternative title, *Hydrophoroi* ('Water-carriers'), a name that would emerge from the initial entry of the chorus with *hydriae*.[13]

Part of the presumed awkwardness of bringing libations onstage in this way is that after this the chorus never leaves the performance area. As a result, their props also remain present throughout the play. In my view, this represents an important decision for the *mise-en-scène* of the play. The musical entry of the chorus employs ritual gestures that constitute ritually appropriate offerings to the deceased. Chorus members can place the jars down, move around them, pick them up, pour, put them down again: the choreographic opportunities are significant and offer novelty, an opportunity not shared by any other extant chorus. That novelty represents a theatrical virtue in this play, and adds visual interest to the scene. It also means that visible grave goods remain present at the *thymelē* throughout the play, providing a visual cue that Agamemnon has finally been appeased, even when the action shifts to the palace door.

Orestes and Pylades get out of the way of the chorus (*LB* 21–2), either retreating partway back along the *eisodos*, or moving to the perimeter of the *orchēstra* where they are out of the visual focus but still present in the performance area. My suggestion is that they move downstage to the perimeter of the *orchēstra*, away from the libation bearers emerging from the palace, but there are other possibilities.[14] The choral song (23–83), accompanied by the rhythmic percussion of their fists on their breasts (24), describes the reason for their visit, a night-time vision Clytaemestra has had that indicated chthonic displeasure (33–41). Mother Earth is addressed directly (45 *ō Gaia maia*), and chthonic offerings are associated directly with a will to accomplish Justice (61 *Dikas*).

The role of the chorus is always a challenge when seeking to under- stand Greek tragedy. It is not a direct representation of the poet's voice, nor an onstage 'ideal spectator' to model responses for the audience, but it is a role with a personality that is integrated into the dramatic world. Choruses usually speak from their own perspective, in this case that of female palace slaves, and they can be mistaken. The identity of the chorus in *Libation Bearers* is again profitably read against that in *Agamemnon*: these women have no social authority, but like the elders in *Agamemnon*, they are allied to the well-being of the former ruler, and not to Clytaemestra (81–3). These women claim to be older than Electra (171), and they are also war-captives (75–7), possibly but not certainly those who have come from Troy with Agamemnon. Crucially, a chorus possesses a collective character: it is not the voice of an individual, but a shared voice representing a plurality. When interacting with other characters, one individual may speak on behalf of the group: this is the *koryphaios* (lit. 'head speaker', the chorus leader). While modern productions often divide spoken choral lines between individuals, in antiquity it seems likely that all choral spoken lines in scenes were delivered by the *koryphaios*. That would streamline the rehearsal process considerably, and mean that only this performer would need a script to learn lines: other choristers would not need to know how to read, and musical sections could be rehearsed with a call-and-response technique.[15]

When the song is finished, Electra addresses the chorus in its collective identity. She seeks advice, and her questions outline the difficulty of her situation (84–105). Electra wants to mourn her father, but she is doing so at the insistence of her hated mother, and on that woman's behalf. Is Electra bringing these offerings in some way disloyal to her father – and not just to his memory, but to his continued existence in the Underworld? She beseeches the chorus as friends (100 *philai*) to advise her. The *koryphaios*, speaking for the group, answers, and the exchange between the two women alternates line-by-line, in a common technique in tragedy called *stichomythia*. From lines 108–23 speakers alternate with the completion of each poetic line, which means that spectators familiar with the technique do not need to strain to perceive which character is speaking behind the masks they wear. Curiously, the artificiality and predictability of this device creates a feeling of naturalism, replicating the natural back-and-forth of conversation, even when a thought is interrupted in order to preserve the back-and-forth (as at 118). The advice from the older woman is to make the offerings on her own behalf, even though they have been provided by Clytaemestra – that is, Electra should deliberately subvert her mother's intentions. Whether god or mortal (119), Electra needs assistance, against Aegisthus and Clytaemestra. 'Do you mean a judge [*dikastēn*] or a justice-bringer [*dikēphoron*]' (120) she asks, employing two compounds of *dikē* in the alternatives for help. The implicit answer is both of these: someone who will kill in retribution (121 *antapokteinei*, a verb that Orestes uses of himself at 274).

Affirmed in her decision, Electra prays (165, 124–51).[16] She too prays to Chthonian Hermes (124, unknowingly echoing the earlier prayer at the same location made by Orestes), to Earth herself (127) and to her father (130). Electra describes the hardships she endures, akin to those of a slave (135 *antidoulos*). She prays for Orestes' return (138) and her own dutiful piety (122 *eusebē*, 141 *eusebesteran*). As a separate prayer, she calls on her father for an avenger, a *timaoros* (143), which is the same word used of Hermes (at *Ag.* 514) and of Orestes in the prophecy of Cassandra (*Ag.* 1280, 'For there will come another, an avenger [*timaoros*] for us').[17] As Sommerstein observes, these prayers are distinct, and at this point Electra does not expect a returned Orestes to be that avenger, even though the audience perceives them to be one and the same.[18] And of course, Orestes and Pylades are visible to the audience throughout this speech, somewhere in the performance area, eavesdropping on Electra's prayer.

While the chorus sings a short song (152–63), Electra pours libations on the tomb of Agamemnon. The packed earth of the *orchēstra* receives the liquid.[19] There is no telling how long this is drawn out, or if individual choristers also empty the vessels they carry, or if there are different fluids with different consistencies. Electra's speech had concluded with instructions to the whole chorus to sing while libations (149 *choas*) are poured. The chorus shouts to Agamemnon, even using the ululation *ototototototoi* (159) that Cassandra had used to begin her prophetic utterance (*Ag.* 1072, 1076). Tears fall as liquid hits the tomb (152), and the chorus itself takes up the cry for a liberator to come, a man wielding a spear, bow and arrow (here called Scythian weapons), or a sword (*LB* 160–3).[20] As each vessel is emptied, it is placed on the *thymelē*, thereby creating a visual image of a tomb that has received the ritual it is due. It is an astrophic lyric, one lacking a metrically corresponding passage, and consequently is not formally constrained in any way. This short song, then, accomplishes two functions. First, it identifies the centre of the *orchēstra* not as a generic space (as it had been in *Agamemnon*), but specifically as the dead man's tomb. The offerings become stage decoration, and part of the set. Second, it positively frames the relations of Electra and Orestes within the theological forces that have been mentioned in the play so far. By populating the performance space with these visual markers, the libation bearers signal to the audience that Agamemnon is now appeased and has been properly invoked to assist in the rightful retribution that is to come.

2.2. Recognition Tokens

Aristotle's *Poetics*, in discussing the nature of tragedy, identifies two plot types: simple and complex. A complex plot contains a reversal (*peripeteia*), a recognition (*anagnōrisis*) or both (*Poetics* 10, 1452a 10–22). Later, when talking about the kinds of recognition, Aristotle specifies that in this play, the recognition is accomplished by reasoning (*ek syllogismou*), 'as in *Libation Bearers*: that someone like her has come, and no one is like her except Orestes, and so he has come' (*Poetics* 16, 1455a 3–6). This logical conclusion emerges from Electra's discussion with the *koryphaios* before she is aware that her brother is present. Aristotle simplifies Aeschylus' scene: Electra does not reach this conclusion by reason alone, prompted by the appearance of a lock of hair that matches her own. The exchange in *stichomythia* (*LB* 168–82) leads her to conclude that the lock she has found at the tomb has come from Orestes, but that he has sent it by proxy in honour of Agamemnon (180). In her long speech that follows (183–211), she both convinces herself that it could have come from no other source than Orestes, and discovers a second proof (205 *tekmērion*) in the two sets of footprints which she is able to follow to the location where Orestes and Pylades are hiding, possibly at the extreme downstage perimeter of the *orchēstra*. Wiles suggests that Orestes has earlier removed his shoes in prepa- ration for his offering.[21] If this is so, Electra's precise description of the footprints makes more sense, and there is an interesting visual echo of Agamemnon removing his shoes to walk on the tapestries (*Ag.* 944–5).[22]

Coming face to face with her brother is not enough to convince Electra. Even when Orestes identifies himself (219 'I am he'), and declares that no one is more dear than him to her (219 *philon*, a word used of friend and family), she suspects a trick from a stranger (220 *xen*', a word also applied to foreigners). To convince her, Orestes holds the lock up to his head to show the similarity, and a third proof is presented, some weaving that Electra had made for him years before that he has kept. In Aristotle's enumeration of means to accomplish a recognition, the philosopher includes the use of tokens (16, 1454b20 *sēmeia*), like the lock and the weaving, but he claims tokens are inartistic and overused. In Aristotelian logic generally, *sēmeia* (tokens) are fallible, in contrast to *tekmēria* (sure signs); but the word *tekmērion* is not used in *Poetics*. Aristotle's presentation of *Libation Bearers* is therefore selective, but he wants an example where reasoning is theatrically effective, since (in his scheme) this is the second-best type of *anagnōrisis*.

Curiously, it is precisely the fallibility of these tokens that is noted in a scene in Euripides' *Electra*, written some forty years after the *Oresteia*. An Old Man, physically embodying the previous gener- ation, suggests the Aeschylean tokens are hypothetical indications that Orestes has returned, and Electra responds to each with a ration- alist critique, noting that there is no reason for a woman's hair to look like a man's, that shoe size does not normally indicate consanguinity, and that a childhood garment should no longer fit a grown man

(*El.* 518–44). Though the scene is unusual, it is not quite as scathing as is sometimes made out. Rather, it shows Euripides engaging clearly with Aeschylus' play, which would likely be familiar to Euripides' audience primarily through reperformance (see Chapter 2.4).

The importance of the recognition scene is also to be observed in the large number of vase paintings representing the moment. More than thirty red-figure vases survive depicting the encounter between Orestes and Electra at the tomb. Most of these are from South Italy in the fourth century, which suggests that this play may have been part of the performance repertoire of plays that were remounted in the Greek colonies. (There are also many vases depicting scenes in *Eumenides*, and perhaps the two plays were performed together; the absence of *Agamemnon* in this context is potentially significant.) The earliest vase, now in Copenhagen, is Athenian and dates to the years 450–30, i.e. in the decades after the initial performance of the *Oresteia*. Also from this period is a series of terracotta plaques, once thought to come from Melos, that share much of the imagery from this scene. It is possible that these predate 458, but the argumentation is shaky. If they do, then it would seem Aeschylus incorporates the type-scene into his play; if not, the objects may reflect the performance tradition. I believe the latter is more probable, especially given the subsequent prominence of the specific theme in vase-painting, but in any case, a viewer familiar with the plays would naturally think of them when looking at one of these scenes.[23]

Considering the scene as depicted in these objects also raises some questions about the visual appearance of Aeschylus' stage characters. The 'Melian' plaques show Orestes entering while leading a horse and possibly with some attendants: this seems unlikely for the play as it survives to us, but we cannot discount the possibility that the counterpoint to Agamemnon's triumphant entry in a chariot was accomplished this way (as the prologue may have indicated unambiguously). Perhaps the horse is meant to suggest they have been travelling, as does their headwear. Orestes and Pylades are typically presented wearing either a *petasos* (traveller's hat) or a *pilos* (gently pointed caps that suggests the wearer is a commoner). In both cases, Orestes' return is marked by humble clothing. Further, the hat is drawn back to reveal Orestes' face in many of these scenes. Sommerstein suggests in his stage direction to line 227 that Orestes is here 'slinging back his travelling hat behind his neck'.[24] It would be at this moment that Electra first sees her brother clearly, as the gradual recognition continues. The text is damaged at this point, but the 'unveiling' of her brother's face with this gesture is possible. It is not quite as straightforward as it might seem, however, given that the actor is wearing an oversize helmet-mask. Athenian masks covered the head and included a wig. Even if they were tight-fitting, the use of headgear of any kind would require oversized pieces of costume, and it may be more natural to assume the two simply come into each other's field of vision.

The consistency of the visual representation of the tomb in these illustrations is also significant. A monumental tomb consisting of low steps and a *stēlē* was somehow fixed as the expected means of representing Agamemnon's tomb. The performance of the *Oresteia* may have created that expectation. The regular decoration, with fillets and various vase-shapes, points specifically to the ritual activity of the chorus in their capacity as libation bearers.

Textual issues trouble this passage, and their treatment reveals some of the discomfort modern scholars have felt towards the scene in a world after Euripides. While scholars now accept the three tokens, the deletion of *LB* 205–11 and 228–9 was argued forcefully by Fraenkel,[25] on the assumption that the motif of the footprints was inorganic and was added by an interpolator who particularly enjoyed recognitions. Fraenkel also believed that Euripides' *Electra* 518–44, which presumes the footprints were part of Aeschylus' play, was also intrusive, added by an even later producer. West and Sommerstein both admit corruption throughout this exchange, beyond the usual difficulties of the manuscript: 206 damaged, a line lost after 208 and 237 moved to help fill a space in a line lost after 243. West also suggests a line has dropped after 228, whereas Sommerstein believes sense in this speech can be restored following the order 225–226–228–227–230–229–223. For our purposes, all three tokens should be treated as genuine, and though the text has been damaged, there is little loss of sense in the scene. The anxiety felt by readers of the play is telling, however: it has been easier to assume that the scene was repeatedly rewritten as it was reperformed than to accept that a tragic playwright achieves an apparently non-tragic tone. This is addressed further in Chapter 4.6.

Orestes tries to convince his sister by presenting the third token, a piece of weaving she had made for him as a child with an animal image on it (*LB* 231–4). There is an intimacy in this unique handmade object from his childhood, and we are not to assume (as does Euripides' *Electra*) that Orestes would still be wearing his childhood clothes.[26] This convinces her, and she accepts him (235–45). He is 'dearest' (235 *philtaton*), and is identified as the last surviving kin that she acknowledges: Orestes is her father, mother, sister and brother, an image that echoes Andromache's affectionate words to Hector in *Iliad* 6.429–30. Though the language might read as transgressive, or as a confusion of family ties, its point here is to emphasize that he alone among the living possesses ties of kinship that Electra will honour. Agamemnon is dead; so is Iphigenia (the reference in *LB* 242 to the 'sister cruelly sacrificed' is the play's only direct reference to Iphigenia, and incidentally shows that there are no other siblings, such as Chrysothemis, as in Homer and, later, Sophocles). Electra's hatred of her mother is 'thoroughly just' (241 *pandikōs*), and on her side are Power (*Kratos*), Justice (*Dikē*), and Zeus.

Mention of Zeus prompts Orestes' prayer (246–63), which introduces rich animal and hunting imagery that is central to the play and to the tetralogy.[27] Orestes presents himself and his sister as eagle chicks (247, 255, 258), orphaned when their eagle father was killed by a viper (247–9). Eagles are the kingly bird of Zeus (*Ag.* 114–15, 137), and so appropriate for Agamemnon; Clytaemestra is the viper that kills (*Ag.* 1233). The psychology of Orestes' image is straightforward and easily interpreted. When later the audience learns that Clytaemestra has envisioned Orestes as a serpent (*LB* 527), the inversion of the imagery helps problematize the ethical situation in which Orestes finds himself, troubling the simplistic binary assertion of good/bad, especially when he accepts the identification (549). When in *Eumenides* an argument is presented that a mother is only a vessel for the child, and that the father is the true parent (*Eum.* 658–66), the audience is being asked to accept as true the hypothetical (and tendentious) formulation found here in Orestes' prayer. That too should give us pause. Orestes reminds Zeus of the offerings made by Agamemnon, bargaining for his divine favour. While the audience is encouraged to see Zeus as supporting Orestes' revenge, many parts of this prayer contain hints of ruin for the house. Indeed, devastation is the final image in Orestes' speech (*LB* 263). There is a darkness and bitterness here, which has quickly eclipsed the joy of the recognition experienced a few minutes earlier. The *koryphaios* prompts direct action (264–8), but even this wish contains reference to the cruel torture whereby victims were covered with pitch and burnt.[28] The moment of happiness has passed, and will not easily return.

2.3 The Avenger

The scene does not end with the recognition between Orestes and Electra. The *koryphaios*' wish that Clytaemestra and Aegisthus be burned alive is followed immediately by Orestes expounding on the oracle he has received from Apollo Loxias (269–305). Even the name Loxias points to Apollo as the god of ambiguous oracular speech (*loxa*), and the information Orestes presents is appropriately troubling. Orestes' words articulate his sense of the consequences of his decision.[29]

The first section of the speech pertains to Orestes specifically (269–77).[30] The oracle has ordered Orestes to seek revenge against his father's killers 'in the same manner' (274), an ambiguous phrase that might suggest 'in return' (Collard), 'in revenge' (Sommerstein) or, arguably most clearly, 'by deceit' (Garvie). Orestes' life is in danger, and he risks suffering beyond the disenfranchisement he has experienced by going into exile. Some of this is interpretation on Orestes' part: the audience is not told the oracle verbatim and that allows space for different interpretations between characters. When, later in the play, Orestes again discusses the details of the oracle, he in fact adds further detail, stating explicitly that Apollo said if he enacted revenge, the god would ensure Orestes was free of responsibility for the crime (1029–33). This is new information when it comes, and anticipates the trial of *Eumenides*. At this point, however, Aeschylus has Orestes stress only the negative consequences of not pursing his father's killers. The audience does not know that Orestes has hope of exculpation in the lead-up to the killing. That, indeed, is a crucial element in understanding how spectators are supposed to respond to Orestes.

A vivid description of the physiological consequences of ignoring the chthonic forces is then presented (278–82): the disease described is similar to a kind of psoriasis, which manifests lesions, white scales and pain from swollen joints. It is a disease that is chronic, painful and externally visible.[31] The Erinyes of Orestes' father Agamemnon are the cause of the prospective torment, a weapon from the darkness of the Underworld brought on by blood-kin that have been killed (283–87).[32] The Erinyes bring madness, nightmares, and a humiliating and violent exile (288–90). This leads to a series of social exclusions, from symposia, libations and sacrifices at altars, from hospitality (*xenia*) and friendship (*philia*), and concludes with an image of an unburied rotting corpse (291–6).

This is the first mention of the Erinyes by name in this play, and indeed the first mention of them in the *Oresteia*.[33] That by itself need not be significant, but given that the *Eumenides* chorus consists of the Erinyes of Clytaemestra, it is plausible that Aeschylus is creating some misdirection. Soon another passage will describe the mechanism of revenge in detail, outlining how blood spilled demands blood in return: 'It is indeed law that murderous drops falling to the earth demand more blood; for destruction calls for an Erinys from those who died before, bringing another ruin on top of ruin' (*LB* 400–4). This passage epitomizes the blood-for-blood necessity of the *lex talionis* understanding of revenge: 'it could be said that this is the central theme of the *Oresteia*'.[34] Crimes must be avenged, and the cycle of revenge can continue through generations. The third mention of an Erinys is at 577, where Orestes' deed is presented as the third crime in a series. The fourth mention of an Erinys is the last word in the next choral song, as Orestes prepares to advance into his father's house as the emblem of Justice, Destiny, and revenge (652). Though the passage contains a punning allusion to Clytaemestra (see Chapter 3.3), it, like all previous uses of the word in the play, calls to mind Agamemnon's avenging furies specifically, and not the Erinyes of Clytaemestra.

The cyclical nature of revenge is crucial to the understanding of the *Oresteia*. Near Eastern law codes enshrine the principle of eye-for-eye, tooth-for-tooth (the *lex talionis*; e.g. Exod. 21.23–25) as a means of establishing limits on what constitutes the maximum acceptable recompense for a crime in a world where legal self-help is routinely practiced. Though Athens was a democracy where self-help could be achieved by recourse to the courts, with volunteer prosecutors who were not always blood kin, the audience knows and recognizes the difficulty in achieving satisfaction through the process of revenge. Though the intent of the *lex talionis* was restorative, in practice each act can feel retributive. Any individual cares more about the losses to oneself than about those felt by another. *Agamemnon* and *Libation Bearers* establish this cycle, and show Orestes obliged to exact revenge, even though doing so means committing another crime deserving of punishment. Matricide is not a restorative act, it cannot be, but because Clytaemestra's crime violated the *philia* that is meant to exist between husband and wife, this situation problematizes the 'rule' (*LB* 400 *nomos*, translated as 'law' above). According to Apollo, the Erinyes of Agamemnon demand her blood.

Orestes therefore has a number of motivations driving him (297–305): he mentions Apollo's command, the great grief of Agamemnon, his own exile and disinheritance, as well as the citizens (302 *politas*), who, having been successful at Troy, are currently ruled by 'two women' (304, referring to Clytaemestra and Aegisthus). What will happen to Agamemnon's possessions, and what will happen to Argos, which currently suffers under bad government, point to additional reasons for Orestes' deed. He has many reasons that show the inherent rightness of his act. It is, or at least seems, inevitable, for even if he does not obey the oracle, the deed must nevertheless be done (298). Apollo's prophecy is additionally supported by the prediction of Cassandra in *Agamemnon* 1280–3: 'For there will come another, an avenger for us, a mother-killing sprout, bringing a father's punishment: wanderer, fugitive, exile from this land, he will come bringing the capstone of these ruins for his friends'. Orestes is that avenger, and the description echoes the description of Orestes that Electra had given at 135–7.

Orestes' decision to avenge his father is therefore overdetermined: he obeys Apollo, he honours his father, he helps the city, and he rightly fears the Furies' punishments that include disease, madness and exile. Electra had prayed that Orestes might return (129–41) and for an avenger to appear (142–51). Though the audience knows these two prayers are both to be answered by her brother, Electra does not, until Orestes proclaims himself to be the avenger in this speech. The confluence of forces driving Orestes to this act are powerful, but they are not irresistible. Orestes considers the possibility that someone else might avenge Agamemnon (298). The deed is one he has chosen, and though we do not see the character struggling to make the choice, the reality of his decision has not escaped him.

What Orestes does appear not to consider, and what Aeschylus does not encourage his audience to consider, yet, is that by the end of *Libation Bearers*, Orestes' decision will mean that he is pursued not by his father's Erinyes, but by those of his mother. This is not fair, but life seldom is. This is the dilemma that Aeschylus dramatizes in the *Oresteia*. The cycle of revenge seems unbreakable, even though *Eumenides*, in providing an *aition* of the first murder trial at Athens, will find a way of removing blame from the killer. A means of exculpation is necessary for society to function, but the *Eumenides* trial side-steps many of the genuine difficulties that *Libation Bearers* raises. How an audience interprets that dissatisfaction is not a problem to be faced just yet. The description of the threat posed by Agamemnon's furies also describes the threat of those of Clytaemestra. Orestes will again be driven into exile, and the horrible description of the disease ensures that everyone watching the play experiences a visceral revulsion at this potential result. Crucially, it is not the case that Orestes does not have a choice. This speech makes it clear that he can choose not to avenge his father. It tells the audience specifically what the alternative to matricide is, according to Apollo. Violent and loathsome and repulsive, it nevertheless does remain a choice. Knowing that, and understanding the alternatives, by the end of the speech, Orestes has affirmed his determination to kill his mother.

2.4 Aeschylus in the 420s

Following the initial performance of the *Oresteia* in 458, Aeschylus' plays continued to find audiences. For whatever reason, it became possible to reperform Aeschylean plays in Athens following his death: I take this to mean that one could enter his plays in competition at the Dionysia with a different director (*didaskalos*). Some believe that only in this way could Euphorion, the son of Aeschylus, have defeated Euripides' *Medea* and its tetralogy in 431. In Aristophanes' *Acharnians* 9–11 (425) a character speaks as if he expects Aeschylus to be performed at the Dionysia, an idea still active in Aristophanes' *Frogs* 868–9 (405), when the character Aeschylus claims his plays lived on beyond his death. Newiger has argued that passages in *Clouds* (423, but subsequently rewritten) also show an awareness of *Libation Bearers*,[35] and in the 410s the Orestes-story again becomes prominent in Athenian literature and art. The generation of these details does not require regular reperformance of Aeschylean tragedy, only that it had happened at least once by 425. While skeptics of this tradition are right that this need not mean a decree was formally enacted,[36] there is no good reason to doubt that reperformance at a main festival could and did occur. In addition, plays were reperformed at other festivals and in other cities, eventually being exported as a cultural commodity to the Greek-speaking world. While not provable, it seems to me very likely that at some point in the early-to-mid-420s (before *Acharnians*, and within the recent memory of many spectators) the *Oresteia* specifically was reperformed, directed by Euphorion or by someone else.

As a result, when Euripides and Sophocles in plays post-425 allude to the *Oresteia*, it is the reperformed version with which most spectators will build associations. While there could be a reading public for individual plays at this point, literacy was not so widespread that a playwright could depend on a reading familiarity of any specific dramatic text. This assumption is supported by the uniformity of visual details associated with the production that are at odds with what is thought to have occurred in 458, and the renewed interest in the subject matter in literary and artistic media.[37] An interest in Aeschylus' plays would coincide with a parallel interest in Stesichorus at this time, who in 421 can be cited in a play without naming him and still be understood (Aristophanes, *Peace* 775 and the scholia there).

The most obvious expression of the influence of *Libation Bearers* on subsequent drama is in the two *Electra* plays of Euripides and Sophocles. Both probably dating to the 410s, these plays present the return (*nostos*) of Orestes as a young man and his murder of Aegisthus and Clytemnestra. In both there is an *anagnōrisis* with his sister Electra based on recognition tokens. This provides a rare opportunity for the direct comparison of the playwriting styles of the three named extant tragedians dealing with the same subject matter.[38] The direct comparison constitutes a standard undergraduate essay topic even today. Before considering this earliest stage of the reception of *Libation Bearers*, there are two essential points to be made.

First, the *Electra* plays are part of a larger pattern of the reception of the *Oresteia* in the drama of this period.[39] A disproportionate number of the extant plays focus on the story of the House of Atreus and its intergenerational troubles. A quick survey of these plays shows the extent.[40] In Euripides' *Hecuba* (*c.* 421), Agamemnon is told the plot of *Agamemnon* by the queen of Troy in a prophecy. Euripides' *Electra* (*c.* 418?) retraces the footsteps of *Libation Bearers*. *Iphigenia among the Taurians* (*c.* 416?) follows Orestes, still pursued by Erinyes, as he and Pylades travel to the Black Sea coast and encounter the sacrificed Iphigenia. Sophocles' *Chryses* (post-414?, non-extant) is apparently set during the return journey from the Taurian land with Iphigenia. Sophocles' *Electra* (*c.* 413?) again revisits the action of *Libation Bearers*. Euripides' *Helen* (412) engages with the plot of Aeschylus' *Proteus*.

Euripides' *Orestes* (408) is set immediately following *Libation Bearers*, before and apparently cancelling the possibility of *Eumenides*. Finally, Euripides' *Iphigenia in Aulis* (produced posthumously in 405) is set at Agamemnon's sacrifice of his daughter, presenting Clytaemestra as a doting mother. These plays engage directly with the Aeschylean telling of the myth specifically, and many individual passages appear to reflect the language or thought presented in the *Oresteia*. There are also plays that deal with the same themes but within a different mythological cycle. Euripides has two plays concerning the matricide Alcmaeon: *Alcmaeon in Psophis* (438, produced with *Alcestis*, twenty years after the *Oresteia*) and *Alcmaeon in Corinth* (405, posthumously produced with *Iphigenia in Aulis*, roughly twenty years after the presumed reperformance of the *Oresteia*). It is hard to conceive that these plays operate without creating some sort of intertextual relationship with *Libation Bearers* (and the network of related plays that followed). Even if verbal parallels in the extant fragments of the *Alcmaeon* plays do not show literary debt, the parallels nevertheless seem inescapable.

Second, the *Electra* plays specifically rewrite the myth as it was presented not in the overall tetralogy but in *Libation Bearers* specifically (*Helen* exists in a similar relationship to *Proteus*). That is to say, *Libation Bearers* was seen as an individual play, separable from its larger tetralogy, by the 410s. Again literacy, and the possibility that papyrus rolls might comfortably hold a single play but not a set of four, is one contributing factor, but that does not provide a complete explanation. By 405, characters in Aristophanes' *Frogs* makes reference both to 'the *Oresteia*' (*Frogs* 1124) but also to individual plays, such as Aeschylus' *Seven against Thebes* and *Persians* (*Frogs* 1019–29). In the following century, reperformances of single plays is standard and that view is reflected in Aristotle's *Poetics*, for whom the single play is the presumptive unit of interpretation. *Libation Bearers* was understood both as a stand-alone dramatic work and one that was at the heart of its tetralogy.

Euripides' *Electra* begins at a humble countryside farm and not the palace of Argos. Electra has been married to the farmer in order to distance her and any children from the royal house. Her initial appearance, carrying a *hydria* (water jar) contrasts self-consciously with the *oinochoai* of *Libation Bearers*. Orestes returns with Pylades, and, following a rationalistic debunking of the Aeschylean recognition tokens (*El.* 518–44), a childhood scar on Orestes' brow proves to be the diagnostic marker, an anti-heroic echo of the boar scar recognized on Odysseus in *Odyssey* 19.[41] Aegisthus happens to be nearby, and is killed by surprise while sacrificing to the nymphs. When Orestes and Pylades return from the brutal slaying, Electra garlands them. Clytaemestra then enters on a wagon (itself an echo of Agamemnon's triumphant *nostos* in Aeschylus), having been lured there by the false report that Electra has given birth.[42] She enters the farmhouse and is killed by Electra and Orestes, who then appear on the *ekkyklēma* (see Chapter 4.7). The play concludes with a divine appearance of Castor and Polydeuces on the *mēchanē* (the stage crane), who predicts Orestes' suffering at the hands of the Erinyes. The play preserves the familiar narrative terrain of *Libation Bearers*, but introduces a number of significant variations. As has been mentioned, scholarly discussion has isolated the discrediting of the recognition tokens at *Electra* 518–44, with many suggesting that the scene was added to Euripides' play in the fourth century.[43] Precise verbal echoes between the two scenes strongly suggest that the audience of the tokens-passage possessed a detailed familiarity with Aeschylus' scene, likely through reperformance. The parody is not as scathing as is often claimed, and the case for interpolation, while possible, remains unproved. Whoever the author of the scene was, performance of the scene is intended to trigger a dual awareness in the spectators, inviting direct comparison between this and Aeschylus' scene.

Sophocles' *Electra* again begins with the return of Orestes and Pylades, this time with Orestes' elderly Pedagogue accompanying them. Electra remains in mourning for her father, grieving publicly before the palace door. Chrysothemis, Electra's sister, models a sensible middle course as opposed to the extremes of Electra, much as Ismene does for Sophocles' Antigone.[44] Recognition is accomplished belatedly through their father's signet ring. The central deception in the play emerges not from Orestes but from the Pedagogue, who gives an elaborate but fictional messenger speech narrating the death of Orestes. Orestes then appears holding an urn, provoking a passionate and heartbreaking lament from Electra who here remains unaware of the ruse. The order of the murders is reversed, with Orestes killing Clytaemestra inside the palace while Electra urges him on outside. Aegisthus arrives, sees the corpse on the *ekkyklēma*, and believes it to be the dead Orestes. As Aegisthus pulls back the shroud, he reveals Clytaemestra and realizes the truth. The play ends with Aegisthus being led to his death in the palace. Sophocles' Electra is impassioned and articulate, and her command of speech (*logos*) is set regularly in contrast to Orestes' more impulsive orientation towards action, deed (*ergon*); the false messenger speech of the Pedagogue and the empty urn physicalize the fictional nature of theatrical presentation.[45]

Each version has diagnostic scenes that could be used to identify the plays in subsequent reception texts. The Pedagogue, the urn, Chrysothemis and the death of Clytaemestra before Aegisthus all help distinguish Sophocles' Electra from other dramatic versions. Euripides' farm setting, Clytaemestra's wagon entrance and the killing of Aegisthus while he is sacrificing at an altar are all without known parallel in the earlier mythic tradition. *Libation Bearers* individuates itself with the recognition at the tomb, the extended lyric *kommos*, the baring of Clytaemestra's breast, and Orestes being beset by Erinyes.[46] As it turns out, the first and third of these scenes are foregrounded prominently in the artistic tradition, into the fourth century (see Chapters 2.2, 4.4, and the Appendix). This demonstrates the direct impact of Aeschylus' play in the later Classical period.[47]

It is possible that the reperformance in the 420s was only the first of several new stagings of the *Oresteia* in the fifth-century. I want to raise the possibility (no more) that part of the tetralogy was also reperformed at the Lenaia, at some point between 420 and 406. The Lenaia was another Athenian dramatic festival, and it instituted comic competitions *c.* 442 and tragic competitions at that time or soon thereafter. Sophocles competed there,[48] and it seems that all the best tragic playwrights might have done so. The tragic competition at this time had two competitors on the same day, each with a dilogy – a pair of tragedies and no satyr play. The possibility of a Lenaia reperformance is only a hypothesis, but it provides an answer to certain questions that are otherwise unexplained. If correct, it would mean that this performance would be the one most familiar to the audiences of *Frogs* in 405. Since the performance would be a dilogy, only the two most tightly knit plays would be performed, and that would be *Libation Bearers* and *Eumenides*. This might even be the source of the name 'Oresteia' (first attested in *Frogs*) – a term that I'd suggest more aptly suits just these two plays, but not *Agamemnon* and the lost satyr drama *Proteus*.[49] When Euripides calls for the *prologos* of the *Oresteia* (*Frogs* 1124), he is using language naturally to mean the first words of the dilogy associated with Orestes, rather than 'the first words of the second play in the tetralogy', or that *Libation Bearers* itself had an alternate name. *Frogs* was itself performed (first) at the Lenaia in 405, and so the continuity between festivals is reinforced. This would also help justify the detailed engagement with the prologue (*Frogs* 1124–76), which in this account is now not quibbling about reperformed dialogue from twenty or fifty years earlier. Theatrical activity in Athens was not restricted to the Dionysia, and some of our extant tragedies were almost certainly performed there (and would be part of a different tragic aesthetic, one without satyr plays). A second reperformance of Aeschylus, at the Lenaia, should be considered a possibility.

The tragedies of the fifth century continued to be performed in the fourth. In Athens, a new opportunity was introduced in 386 at the Dionysia for the production of an 'old' tragedy, which is to say one by Sophocles, Euripides, and presumably Aeschylus, who were already being treated as classics.[50] These reperformances, and the exporting of old plays to other Greek cities, gave continued life to these plays. The prominence of *Libation Bearers* in southern Italian red-figure vase painting suggests that Aeschylus was among the repertoire of reperformed tragedy.

2.5 Further Libations

The story of Orestes and Electra continued to be told, and though it was not always the Aeschylean version that was presented, the legacy of *Libation Bearers* continued to be felt. If Aeschylus was the first to present anthropomorphic Erinyes, to give them a distinctly female form, then the embodied furies of subsequent art and literature all derive ultimately from the *Oresteia*. This includes the Fury that torments the ghost of Tantalus in the prologue to Seneca's Latin tragedy *Thyestes* (*c.* 62 CE), in a play that dramatizes an earlier stage of the inherited curse on Orestes' ancestors.

Orestes himself comes to embody the notion of revenge, and when he is so employed, he reflects the spirit of revenge current in the age that creates him. Benoît de Sainte-Maure's *Roman de Troie* presents Orestes essentially as a twelfth-century courtier, but the choice he faces continues to form a dilemma that is insoluble at the human level.[51] While Benoît did not have access to Aeschylus directly but was adapting from intermediate Latin sources, the impact of the *Oresteia* continued to be felt. It is Benoît's hero that stands behind the earliest English revenge tragedy, John Pickering's *Horestes* of 1567.[52] Allegorical figures interact with the human ones, as the playwright uses classical myth to explore English–Scottish relations. The Climactic encounter between mother and son is overseen by a personified Vice:

Clyt. (*kneel down*) If ever any pity was of mother-plaint in thee,
　　　Let it appear, Horestes mine, and show it unto me.

Hor. What pity thou on father mine didst cursedly bestow,
　　　The same to thee at this present, I purpose for to show.
　　　Therefore Revenge have her away, and as I judgment gave
　　　So see that she in order like, her punishment do have.

Vice Let me alone, come on away, that thou wert out of sight,
　　　A pestilence on thee, crabbed queen. I think thou do delight
　　　Him to molest. Come off in haste, and trouble me no more.
　　　Come on, come on. It's all in vain, and get you on afore.

(*Let Clytemnestra weep and go out. Revenge* [i.e. Vice] *also.*)

Pikering's use of rhyming fourteeners is shared by Arthur Golding's translation of Ovid's *Metamorphoses*, also first published in 1567. Subsequent examples of revenge tragedy continued to look to Orestes, and Kerrigan has shown how both Thomas Kyd's *Spanish Tragedy* (*c.* 1587) and Shakespeare's *Hamlet* (1599–1602) draw directly on Pickering's *Horestes*.[53]

A possible source for these plays is Johannes Sanravius' 1555 Basel translation of Aeschylus' 'six' tragedies into Latin. Curiously, *Libation Bearers* is omitted as a separate play, but is included within the translation of *Agamemnon*, since that was how the Aldine edition first printed the Greek text in 1518, cutting *Agamemnon* 311–1066 and 1160–1673.[54] Henslowe's Diary records that on 2 May 1599, playwrights Thomas Dekker and Henry Chettle were paid for a tragedy called *Orestes' Furies*, and later that month for one called *The Tragedy of Agamemnon*. Though neither play survives, the impact of the *Oresteia* as a connected narrative continues to be felt. The vogue for revenge tragedy at this point emerges in Shakespeare's

Hamlet (1599–1602) and *Macbeth* (1606), obviously, and these too may owe something to Aeschylus' play.[55] Shakespeare's success then leads to re-visionings of the Orestes story, such as Thomas Goffe's *The Tragedie of Orestes* (1613–18), which contains elements of both *Hamlet* and *Macbeth* in its depiction of the revenge. Goffe cites Euripides' *Orestes* as a source, and the Aeschylean influence is at best indirect.

Around this time, Thomas Heywood presented the revenge of Orestes at the conclusion of his magnificent five-play cycle, *The Ages*. The first three plays (*The Golden Age, The Silver Age,* and *The Brazen Age*) were produced and published in 1611–13, and provide a mythological survey from the beginning of the world to the death of Hercules. The last two plays, *The Iron Age* parts I and II, were not published until 1632, and their date of composition remains uncertain. The plays deal with the Trojan war and its aftermath, and lack many of the linking features found in the first three *Ages* plays. In *Iron Age* II, Agamemnon returns from Troy and is killed at a banquet. An adult Orestes swears an oath at the end of Act 4, not knowing who has killed his father:

> Hadst thou my weeping sister hand in it,
> If he whom equal (if not ranked above)
> I ever did and shall love, Pylades,
> Were't she whose womb did bear me, where I lay
> Full nine months bedded ere I saw the sun,
> Or the most abject traitor under heaven,
> Their dooms were all alike, and this I vow.

In Act 5, Orestes and Pylades enter the palace in disguise, kill Egisthus and Orestes confronts Clytemnestra. When she protests her innocence, Orestes calls on angels or devils for a sign, and a ghost appears: '*Enter the Ghost of* Agamemnon, *pointing unto his wounds, and then to* Egisthus *and the Queen, who were his murderers; which done, he vanisheth*'. Heywood seeks to entertain, and freely alters his source material to create the effects he desires, which draws on popular theatrical conventions of his day, as well as borrowing from *Hamlet* and *Macbeth*. The intimate association with Electra and Pylades in the oath are included both to heighten the irony of the unknowing Orestes swearing to kill his mother, but also because they were important to Aeschylus.

Aeschylus' plays were not translated into English until Robert Potter's version of 1777, and *Libation Bearers* was not staged in English until 1886, when George Warr's *The Story of Orestes* brought an abridged Aeschylean Orestes to the London stage.[56] Neoclassical interest in the story is also seen in the 1783 Italian tragedy *Oreste*, by Vittorio Alfieri, which expands on the plot of *Libation Bearers*. As it opens, Clitennestra feels remorse for her previous actions, and is distanced from Egisto. Oreste and Pilade return and recognize Electra, and they present the news of Oreste's death to Clitennestra. Pilade delivers an account of Oreste's death in a chariot accident, clearly drawing on the Pedagogue's speech in Sophocles' *Electra*, but Egisto is not convinced, and arrests the two young men. Only after a popular uprising that frees Oreste and declares him king do Egisto and, later, Clitennestra flee. The play ends with Oreste capturing Egisto, killing him and, in a passion, his mother too. The popular insurrection obviously resonates with the American revolution of 1776, a subject about which Alfieri also wrote.

Libation Bearers does not have a rich, independent performance tradition. The earliest performance of the play by itself is apparently an 1868 production by the Saxe-Meiningen Company in Germany. While there have been performances of the play, in annual European festivals[57] and in academic contexts,[58] it is typically presented as part of the larger extant trilogy. As a result the play is often cut. When it was performed as the Cambridge Greek Play in 1921 and 1933, for example, an original-language production directed by J. T. Sheppard, only 622 of the play's 1,076 lines were included in the script.[59] The

1921 production was filmed, making it the earliest recording of a Greek tragedy, but unfortunately all prints have been lost. The large role for the chorus and the dependence upon unseen supernatural forces in the play are additional challenges that need to be met in production. Further, the more developed psychological presentation of Electra in the plays of Sophocles and Euripides, plays that are more obviously self-contained, have made them more likely to be produced in modern times.

Given the large number of plays that survive dealing with this theme, 'alternative' Oresteias have been also developed. In 2009, Canadian poet and translator Anne Carson published *An Oresteia*, with *Agamemnon*, Sophocles' *Electra* and Euripides' *Orestes*: three plays from three playwrights that cover much of the same mythic space as Aeschylus' three tragedies, but omitting Aeschylus' vision for the revenge. This is one example of a larger trend of building a trilogy from three playwrights, as had previously been done with the narrative sequence of Euripides' *Iphigenia in Aulis*, Aeschylus' *Agamemnon* and Sophocles' *Electra*:

> Making Iphigeneia's story a prologue to productions of Aeschylus's *Oresteia*, sometimes with Sophocles' *Electra* substituted for *Libation Bearers*, has also served in some trilogies or tetralogies to humanize Clytemnestra's later murder of her husband and to link all of the women in the family of Agamemnon as victims of patriarchal rhetoric or abuse and active responders to it during a period in which female bonds and mother-daughter relations were attracting increased examination.[60]

The reference to 'tetralogies' points primarily to Ariane Mnouchkine's *Les Atrides*, a ten-hour production of the *Oresteia* preceded by *Iphigenia in Aulis*, produced by Theatre du Soleil in 1990–2, which toured widely. Mnouchkine's vision kept the action of *Libation Bearers* at the forefront. Rich describes 'the high-throttle confrontation between mother and son, as Clytemnestra runs but cannot hide from Orestes, whose monomaniacal pursuit of his prey turns the wooden arena into a bullring.[61]

It is not possible to document the many productions of the *Oresteia* that have been staged in the twentieth century. Important productions at the National Theatre in London have premiered new translations. Tony Harrison's 1981 translation, directed by Peter Hall, presented an all-male cast, in masks, offering the full trilogy in a translation that emphasized alliteration and acoustic effects in the Greek. In 2000, Katie Mitchell's production of Ted Hughes' translation of the *Oresteia* involved extensive cuts to *Libation Bearers*, even with its running time of over six hours. These are but two of the 14 major productions Taplin lists for the second half of the twentieth century.[62]

Burian presents an overview of three adaptations of the story for the modern stage: Eugene O'Neill's *Mourning Becomes Electra* (1931), Jean-Paul Sartre's *Les Mouches* (1943, *The Flies*), and T. S. Eliot's *The Family Reunion* (1939).[63] All of these re-imagine *Libation Bearers* differently. O'Neill self-consciously constructs a trilogy, and the second part, 'The Hunted', insistently presents the psychological integrity of the characters, in a setting transposed to soon after the American Civil War.[64] The play was adapted into a 1947 film (dir. Dudley Nichols). *Les Mouches* recognizes the cosmic scale of Aeschylus' story, and has Orestes and Electra openly defying Zeus and the Furies. Orestes' return to Argos is motivated by a desire to affirm his personal freedom of choice. The presentation of the Erinyes as a swarm of flies powerfully evokes the sense of moral pollution that hangs like a cloud on the city. *The Family Reunion* appears to be a comedy typical of the period, but as the plot unfolds the audience perceives that Harry is being pursued by Furies, visible in the drawing-room window. In the premiere, Harry was played by Michael Redgrave, who also played the Orestes figure in the film of *Mourning Becomes Electra*.

The story has also been adapted to the media of music and dance. Darius Milhaud composed *Les Choéphores* (1919), using the libretto of Paul Claudel, one of three operatic pieces from the *Oresteia. Les Choéphores* was written second (1915), but was the first to receive a public performance (the other parts were not performed until 1927). Each part was longer than the last and required more performers.[65] Dancer and choreographer Martha Graham's adaptation of the *Oresteia*, like Euripides' *Orestes*, is set directly following the events of *Libation Bearers. Clytemnestra* (1958) begins in the Underworld, and Act II presents the slaying of Clytemnestra and Aegisthus in flashback. Fabric and nets and crimson scarves and gauze curtains and cloaks: the production is filled with textiles and fabrics that lend a sensuousness and materiality to the performance. As in Aeschylus, the same dancer (Bertram Ross) played Agamemnon and Orestes. Graham's source material included American poet Robinson Jeffers's recounting of the story in his 1924 free-verse drama, *The Tower Beyond Tragedy*, which, under the influence of Sophocles and Euripides, keeps Electra active in the play until the end. The epilogue of Graham's dance has Clytaemestra embrace Orestes, in an act of apparent forgiveness. The Underworld scene is overseen by Athena and Apollo, the two Olympian gods who appear in *Eumenides*.[66]

The story of Orestes has even been adapted as a spaghetti western. *Il pistolero dell'Ave Maria* (1969, dir. Ferdinando Baldi), released in English as *Gunman of Ave Maria* or *The Forgotten Pistolero*, covers the events of *Libation Bearers*, showing the events of *Agamemnon* in flashback. After a Mexican general is killed by his wife, the general's son Sebastian and his nurse go into exile, and return fifteen years later to exact revenge. By this time, Anna's interest in her lover Tomas have disappeared, as in Alfieri's *Oreste*. The score by Roberto Pregadio is haunting and memorable, and the film ends with the house consumed by flames, a visual spectacle that redeploys Aeschylus' imagery of light and dark.

The impact of *Libation Bearers* extends far beyond these specific examples, however. Aeschylus' play has shaped subsequent expectations for how a trilogy of three connected narratives should cohere. Without the darkness of *Libation Bearers*, Tolkien's *Lord of the Rings* would have no *Two Towers* (1954) and *Star Wars* would have no *Empire Strikes Back* (1980).

3

Chorus and Character

Throughout the fifth century, the chorus was the defining element of the Greek tragic theatre.[1] The complex poetry of the choral songs is at times tortuous to disentangle, and the poor state of the manuscripts of the play occasionally prevents knowledge of the words, let alone their intended meaning. The audience experience of these songs was of something sung and danced. Words, imagery, rhythm, melody, and gesture all combine to create the effect of the chorus, and modern readers are impoverished when given only a fraction of the theatrical resources that would have originally been available. Choreography and instrumental scores have been lost completely. Nevertheless, a few assumptions allow us to understand some features of Aeschylus' poetic architecture in *Libation Bearers*.

Choral music in tragedy was typically strophic: it was organized in short, paired stanzas that are metrically identical (or virtually so): the *strophē* ('turn') and *antistrophē* ('counter-turn'). Further, this metrical equivalence largely corresponded to a musical equivalence, so that the melody played by the *aulētēs* (*aulos*-player) was the same for both parts of a strophic pair, which in turn suggests that there was a choreographical correspondence as well. This correspondence need not have been so rigid that an *antistrophē* was always danced with identical gestures and movements as the *strophē* (first clockwise, then counterclockwise, perhaps[2]), though at times it may have been this close. Rather, moments will have been largely similar, and consequently the poetry creates resonances – visual and aural 'echoes'– that could be exploited in performance. As a result, though we do not know the notes played, or the tempo, or the accompanying gestures, it is possible to observe where some correspondences are created. This analysis is necessarily limited, but every effort to understand the performative dimension of the chorus is repaid.

The melody of every choral pair is unique, composed for that precise lyric passage and not ever repeated again. Music was provided by an *aulētēs*, playing an *aulos*, a double-reeded instrument with two pipes. The tragic *aulētēs* was a professional musician, who stood on stage but was (by convention) not part of the dramatic world being created by the play. The pipe music set a pitch and also provided tempo, rhythm and melody, and gave a richer aural texture to the choral songs.[3]

Recalling the initial entry song (*parodos*) of the serving women (*LB* 23–83), we see that it consists of three strophic pairs and an epode: that is, four unique melodies, the first three of which are repeated. This can be notated with Greek letters to show the structural correspondence: A, A′, B, B′, Γ, Γ′, ep. (i.e. *strophē* A, *antistrophē* A, *strophē* B…). The chorus emerges with visible signs of mourning that are verbally identified (A = *LB* 23–31): they carry libations, their cheeks gashed, their clothing rent, all of which suggests a recent death being properly mourned. If the audience asks whose death it is, the answer comes in the *antistrophē* (A′ = *LB* 33–41): a woman has had a dream that chthonic forces were angry against 'the killers' (41).

As a new melody begins (B = *LB* 44–53), the lyrics mark a paradox: a *charin achariton* (42: 'a thankless thank-offering') is sent by Clytaemestra, the *dustheos guna* (46: 'woman in bad relations with the gods', and cf. 525). The negating particle *a-* (the 'alpha privative') in 44 *achariton* is echoed in the corresponding line in B′ by three alpha privatives, as holy reverence is described as 'unconquerable, invincible, impregnable' (54–5 *amachon adamaton apolemon*). The emphatic nature of this triplet may recall the description of Helen at *Ag.* 689–90. The fear expressed in 46–7 (*phoboumai*) is repeated at a metrically corresponding point in 57–8 (*phobeitai*), as the chorus' personal anxiety is echoed by an unnamed individual, whom some spectators will know to be Clytaemestra, who has suffered bad dreams (as B′ picks up the theme of A′). The palace survives in a metaphorical darkness since the death of Agamemnon (49–53), and the chorus must await the coming of Justice (61 *Dikas*), which can be in the light, in twilight or at night (in the metrically corresponding 61–5).

As the third melody begins (Γ = 66–70), the darkness of blood soaking into the Earth presages an ongoing sickness for the one responsible for a crime. It is a short *strophē* with a clear hope of punishment for murder. Murder is positionally echoed in Γ′ (71–4) with a similar desire for the one who violates virginity, or perhaps commits adultery (71 *numphikōn* could suggest either). The third strophic pair might therefore be alluding to the murderous Clytaemestra and the adulterous Aegisthus, both of whom will be killed (though the chorus does not know this at this time). It is not an unproblematic association, however. The violation of virginity, at a point that has already been tainted by images of blood in the corresponding passage, might equally indict Agamemnon, whose sacrifice of Iphigenia had been described in the *parodos* of *Agamemnon* (*Ag.* 184–257). In that case, the previous reference to the ongoing sickness of a murderer is equally if proleptically fitting for the young Orestes. Do the waters of Γ′ wash away the blood of Γ? Aeschylus does not say, and the clear meaning of the words (despite some roughness in the surviving text) fails to attach unambiguously to particular individuals. Rather, they allusively shift between past crimes and future ones.

When the audience hears a fourth melody begin, it is not clear that the stanza will not receive a contrapunctual *antistrophē*: it becomes an 'epode' only when there is no repetition of the melody (ep.: 75–83). This effect can be like winding a spring but giving it no release, creating an unresolved tension in the scene that follows. Here, however, the chorus members think of their own capture, and their own continued existence as slaves. The epode serves to point the audience towards Electra (who begins to speak at 84), a woman able to resist Aegisthus and Clytaemestra while the servants must defer, regardless of whether their masters do right or wrong (78 *dikaia kai mē dikai'*). Justice maintains social order just as it maintains ethical norms and due reverence to the gods. The *parodos* sets out these tensions but makes no effort to resolve them, as the song prepares for what is to come.

Libation Bearers has five strophic choral songs, including the parodos. An overview of the choral songs is presented in Table 1. Thinking about the structure of Aeschylean choral lyric is difficult but necessary to appreciate Aeschylus' poetic accomplishment.

From this discussion of the *parodos*, we can begin to identify some of the elements that created theatrical interest during the performance of a lyric passage. Metrical variety attests to musical variety: while consideration of the specific metres used might point to certain melodic or tonal associations, it is unhelpful to push such associations too confidently. With the melody comes a rhythm and a tempo that can vary from *strophē* to *strophē*. The combination of voice and *aulos* will often be in agreement (typically vocal and instrumental melodies will have matched), but harmonies and musical flourishes

Table 1 Strophic choral songs in *Libation Bearers*

23–83	parodos	A, A', B, B', Γ, Γ', ep.	
306–478	kommos	(see Table 2)	(Chapter 3.1)
585–652	stasimon	A, A', B, B', Γ, Γ', Δ, Δ'	(Chapter 3.3)
783–837	stasimon	A, mes α, A', B, mes β, B', Γ, mes γ, Γ'	(Chapter 4.2)
931–71	stasimon	A, mes α, A', B, mes β, B'	(Chapter 4.4)

are always possible, as is the interplay of voices, with individuals being answered by a group (or the reverse). The elaborateness of choral dance, with gestures that can compliment either the *strophē* or the *antistrophē* (or perhaps both) can help reinforce thematic echoes intimated in the lyrics sung. The visual effect of a dozen dancers, in costumes and assuming a dramatic identity (which itself plays against the contrasting role of citizen men that had been adopted in the previous play, and the roles of Erinyes and satyrs that the chorus will adopt in the next two plays) demonstrates a dramatic range of character. Individual melodies may also evoke other familiar but non-dramatic musical traditions (wedding hymns, funeral dirges, sympotic verse, etc.). Stage properties may further enhance some of the dances, as the vases carried by individual choristers doubtless did here. The content of the poetry, found in the surviving words of the text, is part of the effect of the choral lyric, to be sure: but it is not the only part, and for some spectators, other features will be perceived as dominant.

3.1 The Great *Kommos*

The song at *LB* 306–478 is a musical masterpiece, complex and revelatory in its design, that would be recognized in performance for its magnificent grandeur. It is a *kommos*, a kind of ritual dirge marked by the regular 'beating' of the breast by its singers. In this case the dirge is for Agamemnon, offering him the honours that he did not receive when he was killed. In discussions of tragedy, *kommos* is also used to describe a song that involves a lyric dialogue between the chorus and one or more characters, where it need not be funereal (the word *amoibaion* is also used for a lyric exchange between two actors or an actor and the chorus). Both senses of *kommos* are operational here: Electra, Orestes and the *koryphaios* all have discrete parts, and the alternation between single and multiple voices further enhances the dramatic effect, as the elaborate architecture of the song showcases three soloists in lyric dialogue with the chorus. There is, frankly, nothing this elaborate surviving elsewhere in Greek literature. There are many disputed readings of individual words, and it is dangerous to place too much trust on the received text. Since the song represents roughly one-sixth of the play (in terms of line numbers), it is important to engage with it directly despite the many obstacles.

The *kommos* is 'at once a [*thrēnos*] for Agamemnon and an invocation for his ghostly aid'.[4] Scholarship has been divided on the dramatic function of the *kommos*. Before the song, Orestes has returned to Argos in order to kill in retribution (274 *antapokteinai*) 'the two women' (304, i.e. Aegisthus and Clytaemestra). The song does not convince Orestes to do his deed, but it deepens his understanding of the coming act. Conacher subtly sees the *kommos* as 'marshalling all the motivations and forces (human and supernatural) for the undertaking and execution of the dread deeds of vengeance'.[5] There is no single dramatic purpose to the *kommos*: its grand scale and poetic richness exceed any single reductive explanation. As an integrated part of the play, the audience experiences the song as a process, which takes Orestes and Electra from mourning to revenge, together as a pair.[6] It accomplishes a number of specific purposes, among which I would emphasize the following:

1. Agamemnon is properly laid to rest. His burial had been deprived of adequate mourning from the community. Here, his next of kin (two children) and the women of his household (represented by the servants) offer the proper lament due to the dead king.

2. Electra transforms her mother's gifts of appeasement into an offering for revenge. This is a subversive act, undermining the

power of Clytaemestra without her knowing it, and damaging the queen's relationships with supernatural forces.

3. Orestes faces the specific horror of matricide, apart from the general determination of revenge killings. There is a significant musical shift in the *kommos* when Electra first says 'mother' (422 *matros*; she repeats the word at 430 *mater*). While Orestes does not bring himself to say her name or use the word (this is postponed until line 899), the psychological impact of the word on both Electra and Orestes can be observed.

4. Agamemnon's spirit is fused with Orestes' desire for revenge. Conacher builds on Lesky's understanding that the attention of the song vacillates between Agamemnon and Orestes: 'the varied songs of the kommos are designed to affect now the spirit of the dead King and now the emotions of his living avenger'.[7]

5. Independent of the characters, Aeschylus presents human and divine motivations alongside each other, challenging the spectator to accept that both are operating independently, scrutable and inscrutable in parallel.

6. The song naturally continues and extends the image clusters found throughout the *Oresteia*, including the contrast between light and dark (320), nautical imagery (391–3), blood (400–2) and animal imagery (420–2).

7. Aeschylus is also presenting a lyric masterpiece which stands on its own as the musical centrepiece of the *Oresteia*. It serves as a technical showcase for the poet's artistic achievement, and will have been the performative highlight for the cast.

This is not a complete list, but this range of functions demonstrates some ways in which the song operates within a larger artistic design.

To begin to understand the *kommos*, it is necessary to consider its unparalleled complex poetic architecture. This can be daunting, and is not helped by the traditional divisions of the song into eleven

strophic pairs positioned irregularly. In what follows, I have relabelled
the parts in a way that I find clarifies the song's design; a diagram at
the end of this section (Table 2) presents the entire *kommos* as I see
it, with line numbers and traditional labelling. Even in the song-
culture of Athens, the scale of this passage is without parallel, and
Aeschylus' original audience would also have struggled to interpret
it in performance. Further, there are some questions of attribution
(who speaks or sings a particular section), in addition to significant
textual issues arising from the poor state of the manuscripts. Like
other lyric *kommoi*, there are sung portions both for the chorus and
for individual characters, in this case Orestes and Electra. Further,
if anapests are delivered by the *koryphaios* alone, speaking (or
rather chanting) on behalf of the other choristers, it would allow
one individual to set the pace for the entire song and increases the
diversity of voices. Anapests are often unthinkingly called 'marching
anapests' because their predominant rhythm (*da-da-dum, da-da-
dum*) could be used for regular, formal movement, and because they
are often found at the beginning of choral entry-songs, including
Agamemnon 40–103. Marching is not a necessary association,
however, and it is best not to assume a particular tenor of movement
with any metrical form. Unlike many Greek metrical forms, anapests
occupied a regular beat (they are isometric). The *koryphaios* might
be supported, for example, by the entire chorus beating its chest,
providing a regular pulse in order to regulate the song's overall effect.

The *kommos* begins with four units, each comprising anapests, a
strophē, a mesode and the corresponding *antistrophe* (*LB* 306–422).
We saw an 'epode' at *LB* 75–83, a sung passage that followed the final
strophic pair but which did not have a corresponding *antistrophē*.
A 'mesode' behaves similarly, but is positioned between *strophē*
and *antistrophē*. It is not a technique widely used in extant tragedy,
but it will be used twice in later songs in this play (*LB* 783–837 and
931–71). The mesodes possess a melody that is distinct from the

Table 2 Structural diagram of the *kommos* (*LB* 306–478).[8]

	metre	speaker			trad. label
306–39	anap.	*koryph.*			
	A	Or	Agamemnon		1/α
	mes α	Cho			2/β
	A′	El	Agamemnon		1/α′
340–71	anap	*koryph.*			
	B	Or	Agamemnon		3/γ
	mes α′	Cho			2/β′
	B′	El	Agamamnon		3/γ′
372–99	anap	*koryph.*			
	Γ	Or	Zeus		4/δ
	mes β	Cho			5/ε
	Γ′	El	Zeus		4/δ′
400–22	anap	*koryph.*			
	Δ	Or	Underworld		6/ζ
	mes β′	Cho			5/ε′
	Δ′	El	Underworld		6/ζ′
423–55	E	(a) Cho	423-28		7/η
		(b) El	429-33		8/θ
		(c) Cho	439-43		9/ι′
		(a′) El	444-50		7/η′
		(b′) Cho	451-55		8/θ′
		(c′) Or	434-38		9/ι[9]
456–65	Z	trio			10/κ
	Z′	trio			10/κ′
466–78	H	Cho			11/λ
	H′	Cho			11/λ′
	anap.	*koryph.*			

strophic pair within which it is situated. It emerges that the mesodes are themselves corresponding, and so the first and second share a metrical shape (and melody and choreography), as do the third and fourth. The four units are therefore properly seen as two pairs, with

each unit in four parts: anapests chanted by the *koryphaios, strophē*
sung by Orestes, mesode sung by the chorus and *antistrophē* sung by
Electra. Brother and sister sing in response to one another, while the
chorus and *koryphaios* drive the momentum forward.

The first two units are focused on Agamemnon. The initial
anapests (306–14) encompass the theological picture that has been
established already: the *koryphaios* calls on Zeus and the Fates
to preserve Justice, through the inexorable law of 'the doer must
suffer' (313 *drasanti pathein*). When Orestes calls on his father
directly (A = 315–22), Agamemnon is nearby, housed in the tomb,
but at the same time utterly remote, in Hades, creating a paradox
that suggests he is unable to assist his children.[10] The chorus (mes.
α = 323–31) encourage Orestes, and suggest that Agamemnon might
appear (328). Electra also despairs when she addresses Agamemnon
(A′ = 332–9), perceiving both Orestes and herself as suppliants
seeking protection at the tomb (336). As the second unit begins, the
anapests of the *koryphaios* (340–4) stress the transformative power
of song, how a funerary *thrēnos* can become a celebratory paean
(342–3). Properly, a paean is a hymn to Apollo, and it is possible that
Aeschylus subtly anticipates Apollo's later involvement in Orestes'
story with this word.[11] The second strophic pair has the children
each make an unrealized wish about Agamemnon's death: Orestes
(B = 345–54) that he had died in battle at Troy; Electra (B′ = 363–71)
that Clytaemestra and Aegisthus had been killed far from home, and
Agamemnon still lived. Between these two prayers, the chorus sings
the mesode (mes α′ = 355–62, metrically equivalent to the one at
323–31), which pictures Agamemnon ruling in the underworld as
he did on earth. This correspondence is unexpected, and therefore
invites the audience to create associations with the ideas presented.
The two mesodes resonate with each other not only musically, but
in their idealized presentation of post-mortem existence, imagining
regal honours and the ability for Agamemnon to return and assist

his children. The anapests are practical theological statements; the mesodes are hopeful. No one picture is 'right', but contrasting views co-exist and lack integration except in the various interpretations of individual speakers. The focus of these first two units, though, is always Agamemnon.

The next two units articulate a tension between Zeus and the Underworld. In the first, the *koryphaios* begins (372–9) by offering a check on the idealized dreams of Electra: Agamemnon's allies are also dead and the impious hands of those in power (377–8) remain. Zeus sends up ruin from below, Orestes declares (B = 380–5); Electra demands justice instead of injustices (398 *dikan d' ex adikōn*) from Zeus and Earth and other chthonic forces (B' = 394–99). Electra's redoubled cry *pheu pheu* (396) echoes precisely Orestes' earlier double invocation of Zeus (382 *Zeu Zeu*). Between these paired solos, the chorus frames its emotional response, daring to articulate its desire for victory over Clytaemestra and Aegisthus (mes. β = 386–93). In the fourth unit, the *koryphaios* again describes the operational nature of revenge (400–4), that when blood is spilled, slaughter summons a Fury (402 *Erinun*). This resonates with the previous sequence of five anapestic lines (340–4), where the lament was a kind of paean: an association is developed, if only indirectly, between Apollo and the Erinyes. Orestes addresses the Underworld rulers directly (Δ = 405–9), but again introduces Zeus by name, suggesting that he sees a connection between the Olympian king and the chthonic forces that hold his father. The chorus' emotional response to Orestes' piteous cry (mes. β' = 410–17) introduces a note of despair in contrast with the hope it had articulated earlier in the corresponding mesode. In the passage that corresponds to Orestes' direct invocation of supernal powers (Δ' = 418–22), Electra instead considers what other pressures have been caused by her wolf-like, fawning mother (420–1).

The mention of the word 'mother' (422 *matros*, repeated by Electra at 430 *mater*) proves transformative and upsets the rhythm established in the *kommos* so far. The fifth unit, E, consists of six short stanzas, three strophic pairs, that appear in the manuscripts as follows:

(a) Lines 423–8:   the Chorus strike their breasts in lament, explicitly recognizing the *kommos* form;

(b) Lines 429–33:   Electra condemns her mother for the lack of a proper funeral;

(c) Lines 434–8:   Orestes declares that she [Clytaemestra] shall pay, the gods working with his hands;

(c') Lines 439–43:   the Chorus describes how Agamemnon was mutilated before he was interred (the brutal verb 'to armpit' someone powerfully suggests the violence and dishonour involved);

(a') Lines 444–50:   Electra describes her subsequent treatment;

(b') Lines 451–5:   the Chorus urges Orestes to remember this treatment and to undertake the revenge for Agamemnon's sake.

Disorder erupts as this news is revealed: half of each pair is delivered by the chorus, and the other half by either Electra or Orestes; at the same time there is no consistency about whether the Chorus or a soloist starts a strophic pair, nor is there a means by which an audience can anticipate the melody, since strophic response atypically does not provide any satisfaction or closure. We can represent this order as **Ab c | C aB**, capitalizing the speeches of the chorus to show the irregularity. This loses symmetry, but the presence of any musical repetition among the irregular responses does suggest an effort to regain it: 'Aeschylus is developing order and disorder in musical form as a theme'.[12] Almost every scholar discussing the *kommos* preserves this disorder, but there is a lot of protest,[13] principally against Schütz's proposed transposition of lines 434–8 after 455.[14] His solution yields the pattern **AbC | aBc**, two metrically corresponding units with alternation between the Chorus and a soloist.[15] Such an alteration of the text gives Orestes the last word, replacing the responses given by his sister in the alternation with his sister.

Arguments concerning this transposition, on both sides of the debate, link an argument about structure with an interpretation of Orestes' psychology, suggesting that delaying a response until after 455 means Orestes' words represent a decision at which he has arrived over the course of the *kommos*.[16] I contend this conflation of arguments is artificial, and one can believe that increased structural order is desirable, more clearly syncopating multiple and single speakers, without committing to a view that Orestes needs moral or psychological strengthening. Indeed, this suggests that Orestes is re-affirming a decision he has already made, concluding this section (E) with the striking use of the rhetorical figure of anaphora (436 *hekati men daimonōn, hekati d' haman cherōn*, 'with the help of the gods, with the help of my hands'). In a different proposal, Sommerstein argues that lines 434–8 fit better after 443, when Orestes first receives the additional news of his father's mutilation.[17] This preserves the received pattern of stanzas (yielding **Ab C | c aB**) and means Orestes' shout in 434, *oimoi* (left untranslated by Sommerstein) is now seen as a response to the news that Agamemnon's body was mutilated. Further, Orestes' speech is the first time that strophic responsion is introduced in this sequence: he is therefore bringing order to the uneven song, which the next two speeches also attempt to do.

The *oimoi* is not an interjection, and does not start the line as a sudden outburst as we might expect (cf. 405, 429). Instead, it is almost parenthetical, the fifth and final word in the line, as Orestes heaves a sigh to himself having at last voiced the question, 'Where can one turn, O Zeus?' (407). The answer he gives is not sudden nor heated, but it repeats his resolve with full knowledge that it is simultaneously right and wrong. The subject of the verb 435 *teisei* ('she shall pay') is left unspoken, but Orestes' meaning is clear wherever the speech is placed. The chorus has equated Agamemnon's work with

that of Orestes (400–4, 439–43, 451–5), and both will be active in
the revenge. The audience especially perceives this because the same
actor likely plays both roles: the characters are fused. Both proposed
rearrangements (placing 434–8 after 443 or after 455) are improve-
ments on what is in the manuscript, and although the implications for
the kind of disorder created in each of these proposals are different,
both clearly mark the importance of Orestes' only speech in this
section. Though scholarship has typically insisted on the manuscript
order, once a stanza is shown to be dislodged (as Sommerstein
has done), the possibility of more regular order, following Schütz
(**AbC | aBc**) must be considered plausible. Whatever the answer,
these six speeches are tightly bound together and are presented as a
single unit (E) in Table 2.

Order is restored, and there is a shared perspective shown in the
short strophic pair that follows (Z, Z′), which blends three voices:
a line from Orestes, a line from Electra and three from the chorus
(456–60), a pattern which is then repeated (461–5). The first stanza
presents a direct appeal to Agamemnon (cf. 306–71); the second
calls on the gods and Justice and Fate (cf. 372–422). Chthonic and
Olympian powers combine as Orestes undertakes his revenge. He
remains undeterred, despite the warnings from the chorus, and has
now confronted the reality that achieving revenge for his father, even
with all the gods supporting him, means killing his mother. Line
461 presents this conflict with concise precision: *Arēs Arei xumbalei,
Dikai Dika* ('Ares clashes with Ares, Justice with Justice'). It is inevitable that one follows the other; there can be no escape. Nor is it clear
that Ares, here an embodiment of bloody violence, is to be seen as
fully distinct from the justice of revenge by self-help.

The *kommos* ends with a final strophic pair from the chorus (H,
H′ = 466–75). Perhaps the chorus unites with the voices of Electra
and Orestes; perhaps the siblings singing the *antistrophē* in response
to the chorus' *strophē*: the relief for the wound (471 *emmoton*, a

medical term meaning 'tent', inserted to keep a wound open so it can bleed) will come from the house (represented by the *skēnē*). Orestes is to be the avenger: this is the song (475 *hymnos*) of the chthonic gods. A coda of three anapestic lines (476–8, and so the *koryphaios* again speaking alone), repeats the prayer to the blessed chthonic powers (476 *makares chthonioi*): asking them to send help to the children, for victory. That final word, 'victory', resounds as a note of hope as the music stops and the two siblings continue their prayer in spoken iambics.

This final choral pair (*LB* 466–75) is arguably the most read passage in all of Greek tragedy, because of its use as an epigraph to a novel for children, J. K. Rowling's *Harry Potter and the Deathly Hallows* (2007).[18] Rowling's quotation is presented without speaker indications, but identifies the classical source (she cites Fagles's 1984 translation). Readers are invited to identify the wound, the cure within the house and the urgent summons of chthonic forces within the context of the Harry Potter series. At the same time the author telegraphs to those familiar with the *Oresteia* the narrative darkness that she intends to pursue, intimating larger themes of kin-killing and prophecy.

By the end of the *kommos*, what then has changed? Nothing, and yet everything. All supernatural forces are now united behind Orestes in his revenge: Agamemnon, chthonic forces, Zeus, Justice and the gods. At the same time, Orestes has come to a new understanding of his decision, even if he still has not spoken the fatal word 'mother'. Agamemnon has been mourned, and his posthumous treatment revealed. Offerings have been made, confounding Clytaemestra's design. And mourning has been transformed into a renewed desire for revenge, with victory expected.

Modern productions of the *Oresteia* or of *Libation Bearers* help readers appreciate the scale and scope of the *kommos*. The 1981 National Theatre production in London, directed by Peter Hall and translated by Tony Harrison,[19] presented a magnificent, masked, all-male cast focused on the grandeur of the Aeschylus' story: action was heavily stylized as the aggressive and image-rich translation brought driving patterns to the words of the actors with rhyme. There was not a lot of movement but the tempo varied greatly throughout the *kommos*, with Orestes and Electra often quicker and more insistent than the chorus, which distributed lines between individuals or groups of speakers freely to provide an added sense of aural movement. The *kommos* in this production occupies eight-and-a-half minutes of the play's 67-minute run time. In the 2014 Greek-language production of the play at Barnard College, the contrast between chanted anapests and sung stanzas was particularly striking.[20] Here the *kommos* lasts 15:30 minutes of its 95-minute run time. In both productions, the *kommos* is a substantial and crucial component of the play's wider impact.

3.2 The Ghost and the Dream

The music of the *kommos* stops, but Orestes and Electra, with Pylades at their side, continue their direct address of Agamemnon's ghost at the tomb. It is a powerful, insistent scene, as both characters invoke chthonic forces to their aid. For its poetic technique, the scene can be compared to Cassandra in *Agamemnon*, whose lyrics (*Ag.* 1072–1177) are followed by an exchange in spoken iambics (*Ag.* 1178–1330). The spoken part of this scene is much briefer however (*LB* 479–509), and Sommerstein's stage direction at 489–96 suggests Orestes and Electra are on their knees, 'beating the ground with their hands'[21] in time to the line-ends of the *stichomythia*, and so continuing the imprecatory tenor of the *kommos*. Electra invokes Phersephassa (490), an Athenian name for Persephone that will call to mind the Eleusinian mysteries for many in the audience, who were initiated in this cult centred at

Aeschylus' birthplace. Eleusinian worship offered a new understanding of the afterlife, which is relevant here, as (perhaps) is the anticipation of Athens in *Eumenides*. Aeschylus reminds his audience of the images seen previously (bath at 491, net at 492–4), and he maintains the precise antiphonal balance of speeches between Orestes and Electra (2 lines each, 3 lines each, 4 single lines in *stichomythia* each, 3 lines each,[22] 2 lines each). Electra is concerned about her eventual wedding (486–8) and presents Orestes and herself as nestlings (500–2, recalling Orestes' presentation of them as eagle chicks at 247–9, 258): 'Send Justice [*Dikēn*] as an ally to your friends [*philois*]' Orestes prays (497).

After the *kommos*, after this, it is reasonable to ask if the audience is expecting Agamemnon to actually appear, in a necromancy. Ghosts had been summoned from the Underworld previously in Aeschylus, following an extended incantation from the chorus: in addition to Darius in *Persians* (472 BCE), Aeschylus composed the now-lost *Psychagogoi* (*Soul-Raisers*), and Io believes the ghost of Argus has returned and pursues her in the form of the gadfly (*Prometheus Bound* 877–86).[23] Sommerstein argues that the audience does expect Agamemnon to appear (after either lines 478 or 496), potentially leaving the audience wondering if his absence signals that Agamemnon did not approve of Orestes' revenge, or perhaps lacked the power to escape the Underworld.[24] Sommerstein calls this a 'negative dramatic surprise' in which 'the expected startles by failing to occur.'[25] He is, I believe, correct that many spectators would reasonably expect the physical, embodied appearance of the ghost of Agamemnon at this point. It is less clear to me that this constitutes an occasion to be startled rather than disappointed. The scene is theatrically challenging because the absence of Agamemnon risks so much, even if it can be formulated in terms of an Aeschylean desire to present a more rationalistic world view.

This problem has not been adequately addressed. Assuming we accept the play's premise that Orestes undertakes revenge that is both just and divinely sanctioned (even if its implications are monstrous), the absence of Agamemnon's visible support risks confusing that message substantially, inviting conflicting interpretations. Dividing an audience can be a powerful theatrical technique, but since it is not subsequently mentioned, it is probably not what is happening here.[26] It would be clearer if the *mise-en-scène* did somehow provide a sense of Agamemnon's long-distance approbation. I can suggest two ways this could be accomplished here, either or both of which could be used. The first involves the physical blocking of the scene, how actors are positioned on stage. If Orestes moves to and stands at the place where Agamemnon is expected to appear (based on whatever theatrical precedents might be shaping audience expectations), the audience is invited to associate him directly with the vengeful spirit of his father. This location will certainly be in and around the *thymelē*, perhaps with Orestes climbing onto it from the 'upstage' (*skēnē*-side) direction. The precise move doesn't matter, so long as it coincides with where the audience expects Agamemnon. Instead of the father, it sees his son, Destiny's sword, honed for the deed, and played by the Agamemnon actor. This would produce an unexpected result, but not so obviously a disappointing one, and one that is interpretable as being a fulfillment of the chthonic prayers. Evocative blocking can provide symbolism to signal a larger meaning to the audience. Second, the *aulētēs* could perhaps repeat a musical strain that evoked Agamemnon's triumphant entry, the anapests at *LB* 476–8 melodically recalling those of *Ag.* 783–809. We do not know to what extent, if any, *aulos* music provided leitmotifs of this sort in tragedy, but such a device could help greatly here. These are admittedly guesses, but something along these lines would help minimize the potential for anticlimax.

The pace of the play now begins to quicken. The iambic portions of this scene (479–584) fall into three segments, each of which involves a different kind of supernatural intervention in Orestes' plot. In the first (479–509), just discussed, Orestes and Electra pray to Agamemnon. In the second (514–550) the *koryphaios* reveals the details of Clytemnestra's dream to Orestes. In the third (554–84) Orestes affirms Apollo's prophecy and reveals the details of his plan. Between these segments are short transitional speeches from the *koryphaios* (510–13, 551–3). Each segment ensures that the audience has a clear sense of the events to follow. Following the first segment, concluding with the prayer, the audience is confident in Agamemnon's support for the revenge action (or so I believe). In the second segment, it comes to a greater understanding of Clytaemestra, her dream, and, as it turns out, Aeschylus' relationship with his sources.

Orestes asks the *koryphaios*, who claims to have been an eyewitness and affectionately calls him 'child' (523), the nature of Clytaemestra's dream. Having been afflicted by night-terrors, the *dustheos gunē* (525 'woman in bad relations to the gods', the same phrase used at line 46) sent drink-offerings for the tomb (*choes*). The details of the dream emerge in *stichomythia*:[27]

> It seemed, as she herself said, she gave birth to a snake … (527);
> … and anchored it in swaddling clothes like a baby. (529);
> She herself in the dream offered it her breast … (531);
> … so that in the milk it drew a clot of blood. (533).

The meaning of the dream is so transparent, and the infant biting the mother, both nursing and attacking, is terrifying and memorable. In certain contexts, both milk and blood are appropriate libation fluids (animal milk, at least), and are particularly appropriate as life-nurturing liquids for chthonic prayer (compare Odysseus' blood offering at *Od.* 11.35–6). The *koryphaios* stresses Clytemnestra's own subjective experience of the dream (527 and 531 *autē*, 'herself'). Neither Electra nor the *koryphaios* interprets the dream. Instead, that function is left to Orestes, who identifies himself as the dream's fulfillment (540–50). For the Greeks, oneiromancy is more effective when the dreamer and the interpreter are separate: dual agency affirms the god-sent understanding that emerges.[28] The chorus is pleased with this interpretation, as Orestes casts aside the established avian/Olympian imagery to see himself instead as a chthonic serpent.[29]

The dream also resonates with Stesichorus' version of Orestes' story. Among the few surviving fragments is an account of a dream of Clytaemestra, in which 'it seemed to her a snake came, the top of its head bloodied, and out of which appeared a Pleisthenid king' (Stesichorus fr. 219). Here, the serpent is apparently Agamemnon and blood pours from the head wound given by Clytaemestra. The 'Pleisthenid king' apparently refers to Orestes as the avenger for the wound (though admittedly the details and larger context remain obscure; and see *Ag.* 1569 and 1602 for earlier references to the line of Pleisthenes). In an almost dreamlike way, Aeschylus preserves the symbols of Stesichorus' account, but redeploys them. For spectators attuned to this Stesichorean parallel, Clytaemestra's snake becomes both Agamemnon and Orestes, united; the blood is that of both his murder and hers, united. The richness of this parallel also points to how much our understanding of *Libation Bearers* would change (and improve) if we possessed Stesichorus' poem. Precisely this sort of engagement, adapting and redeploying imagery to new purposes, would reveal much about Aeschylus' artistic design. Again, there is a symmetry in this section, with the *stichomythia* framed by the *koryphaios* describing Clytaemestra sending libations to the tomb, which in turn is framed by a longer speech by Orestes, as he moves from ignorance of the dream to its truest interpreter.

The third segment of this scene (554–84) consists of a single speech from Orestes, outlining his plan to enter the palace with Pylades by stealth, and kill Aegisthus. He is confident and decisive, apparently revitalized by the ghost and the dream. It is a magnificent speech, and draws together many figures introduced earlier in the play. Electra, for example, has said nothing since *LB* 509, but her constant presence as Orestes' supporter has persisted. At 554–5 and 579–80, Orestes gives instructions for how she can help from within the palace. At 561–4, Orestes describes how he will approach the palace door (561 *pylas*, and 571 *pylōn*) with Pylades, his friend's punning name almost a talisman for gaining admission, as the two adopt a Phocian accent.[30] At 581–2 the *koryphaios* (and, by extension, the chorus) is also given instructions for how she can help.

Orestes describes his plan: he will enter and kill Aegisthus who, as he imagines, sits on his father's throne (571–8). Clytaemestra is not mentioned, though Orestes correctly anticipates the presence of the Doorkeeper and even prepares to insult Aegisthus in conversation if he is not admitted as a suppliant (565–70). This is foreshadowing, obviously, and will prepare the audience for hearing the Doorkeeper's voice when it comes. The description also resonates with an inherited *Oresteia*-tradition, since in artistic representations, throughout the sixth and early fifth centuries, Aegisthus is regularly placed on a throne (sometimes shown at leisure, playing a lyre).[31] Orestes assumes that Aegisthus is in control, lacking the visual sense of him that the audience has from *Agamemnon*, which showed Aegisthus as weak and effeminate (though see *LB* 304). Aegisthus will be killed first, when the Erinys will be given the third drink of unmixed blood (577–8): this theme was established in *Agamemnon*, drawing on the traditional practice of the symposium, in which the third of three libations was poured to Zeus the Saviour.[32] At *Ag.* 246, the imagery was used at Iphigenia's sacrifice, and 'triples' have been present elsewhere (*Ag.* 1386, 1476, *LB* 244–5, with more to come). If Aegisthus' blood is to be the third libation, Agamemnon's is retroactively seen as the second; but what was the first? Iphigeneia, perhaps, or Thyestes if spectators imagine an exclusively male line, regressing the familial curse to a previous generation. That is what the chorus will assume at 1065–74, when trying to make sense of the surprise ending to the play. Either way, Aegisthus' death is seen as a culmination of an ongoing engine of blood-debt fuelled by the Erinyes. Importantly, Clytaemestra is not apparently part of this cycle, and her fate is not specifically anticipated.

Finally, Orestes' speech is interesting for what it reveals about the Olympian gods, particularly Hermes and Apollo. Both of these gods are important to Orestes and his mission, and both shape the nature of the revenge he takes, as seen in Chapters 2.1 and 2.4. Orestes is confident in the oracle he has received (269–70), and here expands on his plan (556–9). He stresses the instructions of Apollo (Loxias) to employ trickery (556, 557 *dolōi*): this is a detail Sophocles adapts in *Electra* (37 *doloisi*), where interpretation of the play hangs on the apparent appropriateness of the use of guile in this way. Certainly, trickery is associated more naturally with Hermes than Apollo, who is described as 'a prophet who has not lied previously' (559). This line is also noticed by the later tradition: Euripides has Orestes say, 'Apollo was a prophet, but he lied to me' (*IT* 711), drawing out the paradox which is implicit in Aeschylus (and see Euripides, *Electra* 1246). The speech ends with a request to 'this one' (583 *toutōi*) to oversee the coming action, with the demonstrative adjective supported by a gesture. At various times, Hermes, Apollo, Agamemnon and Pylades have been thought to be the correct referent here. The verb to oversee (583 *epopteusai*) suggests supernatural vision, which excludes Pylades. The overdetermined supernatural world that has emerged through the *kommos* and this scene invokes all these forces, and possibly (see Chapter 2.1) the stage setting contains some marker to Apollo and Hermes to which Orestes can gesture.[33] Any confusion, however, exists only for us: Orestes' gesture will have been unambiguous in performance. The mention of coming 'contests' (584 *agōnas*) would seem to favour Hermes as the god Orestes intends, recalling his initial invocation of him at *LB* 1.

Apollo nevertheless has an agenda here, and it is one that will become increasingly explicit in *Eumenides*. The god has kept information from Orestes, and Aeschylus has Orestes keep information from the audience (new details will be introduced at 1029–32; see Chapter 4.7). Apollo may be an Olympian, but he is not fully aligned with the will of Zeus. Whatever divine politicking is going on, human inability in the light of divine power, represented here in Orestes' dependence on an oracle to know how best to direct his future, is central for understanding how fifth-century Athenians think about their gods and their own place in the universe. Human inability in the light of divine power is a reality to be faced, and one measure of heroism is how that challenge is met. Divine power is arbitrary, manipulative and sometimes cruel. How we deal with that is one way others can see our character.

3.3 Evil Women

The choral stasimon at *LB* 585–652 is comprised of four strophic pairs (A, A′, B, B′, Γ, Γ′, Δ, Δ′). It is a profound, reflective song that focuses the chorus completely on the thoughts of Orestes and his revenge. It also is an exceptional example of how the chorus can invoke mythological exempla to invite the audience to compare the immediate narrative with other mythological examples. 'The earth breeds many beings that cause terrible [*deina*] fearful suffering …', the chorus begins (585–6), but of all the monstrous things in the world, none is more frightful than men and women living together in a house: 'The homes that couples share are evilly conquered by the passion [*erōs*] that overpowers the female [*thēlukratēs*], both among beasts and among men' (599–601; tr. Sommerstein). The first strophic pair establishes a premise that the subsequent ones will test. The magnificent, ambiguous adjective *thēlukratēs* combines words for 'female' and 'power' in a way that is mysterious and not obviously interpretable on a first hearing. It is probably right to see this stanza as a source for arguably the most famous lyric surviving from Athenian tragedy, the so-called 'Ode to Man' in the first stasimon of Sophocles' *Antigone*: 'There are many terrible/awesome [*deina*] things in the world, but none more *deina* than man ...' (*Ant*. 332–75). Where Sophocles universalizes, Aeschylus offers a corrective to rigid gender divisions: families are broken, and through passion or love (*erōs*) men and women vie for power in a household.

Consider Althaea (B = 602–12), the daughter of Thestius, who caused the death of her son Meleager when she heard that he had killed her brothers. There was a log for which it was fated her son would die when it was burnt. Althaea had kept it since Meleager had been born, but on receiving this false news after the events of the Calydonian boar hunt, she placed it in the fire. This effected her son's death (see Bacchylides, *Ode* 5.93–154). A mother who designs the death of her son is obviously relevant to the dramatic context of Clytaemestra and Orestes, with Althaea's passion placing greater value on her siblings than her own child.

Or consider Scylla (B′ = 613–22), who betrayed and possibly killed her father Nisus. Like Althaea, she is not named, and the precise mythic variant Aeschylus has in mind is not obvious. Somehow she ruins her father when the Cretan king Minos bribes her with a gold necklace (615–17). Again, direct obligations owed between parent and child are upset, in this case more clearly motivated by erotic passion. Scylla, the woman with a dog's mind (621 *kunophrōn*) cut a fated lock of Nisus' hair. Nisus' purple lock preserved him and the city of Megara, and the audience is invited to associate this hair-cutting with that of Orestes at his father's tomb. The situations do not map onto each other precisely, but they share a nexus of images that are clearly evocative.

Or consider the Lemnian Women (Γ = 631–8), who murdered

their husbands and took the Argonauts for lovers. In the light of *Agamemnon*, the relevance of this example is obvious, and Aeschylus spends the *strophē* emphasizing the how they have become a watchword for criminality, 'for no one honours what is hated by the gods' (637). They committed horrors (634 *to deinon*, recalling 586), and their mention here is a counterpoint to Athena's use of the Amazons at *Eum*. 685–90.[34]

Each of these three examples is set in the generation before the Trojan war; they have each become proverbial for the palace servants as they are for the Athenian spectators (602 'anyone may learn …'; 613 'in tales …'; 632 'in a tale …'). Indeed, the chorus invites the audience to consider the appositeness of these examples (638). Given that, I am inclined to accept Preuss's transposition of 623–30 and 631–8, as argued by Stinton.[35] This then creates a priamel, a rhetorical structure that lists a series of alternatives before addressing the main theme: in this case, three mythological *exempla* (woman against son, woman against father, women against husbands) lead to the immediate context (what the manuscripts give as Γ): Clytaemestra and Aegisthus constitute an immediate example that pulls the veil back from the allusiveness the chorus has practiced.

The antistrophe (Γ′ = 623–30) is even more allusive, but it also identifies its subjects unambiguously. A hateful marriage that offends the house (624–5), with a woman plotting against his soldier husband (626–7): the servants deplore the adulterous relationship of Clytaemestra and Aegisthus and the murder of Agamemnon. This is the problem of 'female plotting' (626 *gunaikoboulous*), a word which resonates strikingly with the androgynous presentation of Clytaemestra, whose heart was *androboulon*, 'male-plotting' (*Ag*. 11). Both compounds refer to the queen, but here, set amongst the crimes of other evil women, Clytaemestra's femininity is dominant. It is best not to avoid too much passion in order to maintain domestic harmony, the chorus advises: 'I honour a domestic hearth that is not warmed' (*LB* 629–30). All of the examples involve passions that have gone wrong or been misdirected, and sexual corruption in particular has been referenced in the Scylla example. *Better a hearth not be too hot* proverbially encapsulates the themes of the stasimon.

Now some spectators may reflect that women alone are not responsible for violence in the world. Indeed, for some the example of Althaea might instead evoke Agamemnon's killing of Iphigenia, but with the sexes of the characters switched (or indeed it may evoke the crime Orestes is about to commit); the example of Scylla might also invoke Agamemnon and Iphigenia, with parent killing child instead of the reverse (B, B'). The adulterous desires of the Lemnian women and Clytaemestra were also shared by Agamemnon for Cassandra (Γ, Γ'). This is not what the chorus is thinking, but given the allusive nature of choral song generally, it may be what Aeschylus is thinking: both Iphigenia and Cassandra were invoked in *Agamemnon*, and some spectators are likely to question the appositeness of these examples. Lebeck considers these crimes and suggests they 'give back a looking-glass reflection of the parallel crimes committed by Agamemnon and Orestes, reversed in such a way that woman's crimes come to the fore each time'.[36]

The final strophic pair draws the conclusion: 'This sword' (639) pierces lungs because Justice (641 *Dikas*) has been downtrodden and Zeus dishonoured (Δ = 639–45). Justice (646 *Dikas*) is firm and Destiny (647 *Aisa*) is a swordsmith, and a child will be brought into the house to avenge inherited blood-guilt (Δ' = 646–52). The stasimon's final word, Fury (652 *Erinys*), pulls together the themes of inter-gender and inter-generational crimes, as well as the need for vengeance (the word had previously been postponed until the end of a *strophē* at *Ag.* 749). Indeed, the Erinys is *kluta* (651, 'famous'), using the word that comprises the first part of Clytaemestra's name. All these personified forces – Justice, Destiny, Zeus and the Furies – focus around the image of the child Orestes and his avenging sword.

Orestes and Pylades, of course, are armed with swords. All travellers would carry swords because the roads are wild.[37] And Orestes' sword, forged by Destiny, will pierce lungs (very soon …) in a place where Justice has been trampled and Zeus, god of kingship, dishonoured. Orestes holds the weapon, and he is the child: this is no longer figurative, especially if Orestes is still on stage. It is a brutal, beautiful hymn.

Stage directions must be inferred from the words spoken, and there is a unanimity of opinion at this point, reflected in all major translations, against which I would like to argue. It is usually thought that Orestes and Pylades retire along an *eisodos* when Electra leaves at 584, leaving the chorus alone on stage for the stasimon, and then return along the same *eisodos* and approach the palace door.[38] This view holds that the performance space 'refocuses' from the tomb of Agamemnon to the Palace at Argos (subsequently, the tomb is mentioned at 722–5). This refocusing is more problematic than is generally recognized, since it is not accompanied by an 'empty stage', as at *Eumenides* 234, which allows for the transition from Delphi to Athens.

Orestes has outlined his plans to arrive at the palace with Pylades assuming the accent of a Phocian: this is to be his disguise. Does he alter his appearance further? I believe he does not. There are no special 'Phocian garments' he must put on. He is a traveller who has come on the road with luggage. He and Pylades have the broad-brimmed *petasos* that travellers habitually wore (see Chapter 2.1). He is unknown in Argos as an adult and already looks like a foreigner. No further disguise is necessary. Once this is acknowledged, the need for Orestes and Pylades to leave and return similarly disappears. If they stay onstage, readying themselves at the centre of the *orchēstra* while the chorus allusively sing about the evils women do, then at the final reference in *strophē* Δ to Orestes and the sword of Justice, the meaning of the image becomes strikingly clear. The audience has seen their preparations (however minimal they were), and consequently is in the know, more closely allied to Orestes.

In this light, we should reconsider previous movements: I've suggested that the chorus and Electra make their initial appearance from the *skēnē* which represented the palace, and it was to there that Electra returned at 584. Scholars who assume the scene must 'refocus' over the course of this stasimon often have the characters enter by an *eisodos*, but this creates a needless complication. Electra has to go to the palace on receiving Orestes' instructions, and the clearest indication of where that is can be achieved by having her walk to the visible central door of the *skēnē*. Using an *eisodos* requires the refocusing that others have postulated. With the continuous presence of the chorus, though, this is problematic.

On a non-naturalistic stage without defining or localizing details of setting, the distance that exists between the tomb of Agamemnon and the palace of Argos is not the 10 metres or so that physically separates the two locations in the performance area. The structure of *Libation Bearers* concentrates on these two locations: the tomb of Agamemnon at which the libations are poured, and the doorway to the House of Atreus, which in *Agamemnon* had been represented by the *skēnē* building. As was observed (Chapter 1.3), these are the two points of particular strength in the Athenian performance area because they represent a visual focal point. In isolating these locations, I am not removing opportunities for the creative use of the entire playing space, but I am suggesting that either of these locations can be thought of as 'centre stage' and that actor positions will naturally acknowledge this. For example, in *Agamemnon*, after a long delay, Agamemnon and his retinue arrives on a chariot (*Ag.* 783). He then makes his way into the palace, destroying the tapestries as he walks barefoot to his death (*Ag.* 958–72). My understanding of visual focus means that this pivotal movement involves him walking from a point at or near the *thymelē*, his citizens the chorus scattered around him through the *orchēstra*, to the central *skēnē* door, from one 'power point' to another. This is not particularly controversial: the chariot must stop somewhere in the *orchēstra*, and near the visual focus of all the spectators will be the natural place to allow the audience to understand that Agamemnon has fully returned, accomplishing his *nostos*.

I believe this fundamental movement, from altar to door, is repeated in *Libation Bearers*. Orestes arrives at the tomb of his father, and then proceeds into the house.[39] Indeed, the replication of Agamemnon's fatal march on the tapestries is arguably the central movement of *Libation Bearers*. In his monumental 1977 study arguing for a consistent 'grammar' of entrances and exits, Taplin indicated that following the great *kommos* at the tomb, Orestes and Pylades go offstage (or 'withdraw to one side'[40]) at line 584, and then return as the stage setting 'refocuses' to the palace during the chorus' song at 585–652. This departure of Orestes and Pylades is unnecessary, and it is preferable for the avengers to remain onstage at the tomb during the choral ode.

Two reasons are given for why the male characters need to exit. The first has been discussed. If Orestes and Pylades assume a disguise of some sort, the offstage location provides cover for any alterations to the costume that might occur (561–4). There is no indication that either character speaks in anything other than the standard dialect for tragic speech, which means that saying this is sufficient.[41] Nor is there any reason for a change of costume: the men are already attired as travellers, and since Orestes has not been seen since he was an infant, there is no need to disguise his clothing (despite the third recognition token at 231–2). Further, effecting a costume change risks confusion. Euripides' *Helen* shows the great lengths to which the Athenian stage needs to go to handle an offstage costume change: announcement before the exit that a change will take place; repetition that a change has taken place after the character returns.[42] Without that preparation, an actor leaving and changing costume and perhaps mask risks being interpreted as a new character. In contrast, an alteration to costume (if any) in the sight of the audience risks no confusion at all, since the spectators have witnessed any transformation that took place.

The second reason involves naturalism in the performance space. Scholars no longer assume that elements of a representational set were used. While exceptions do exist, for the most part scenography is neutral and elements of the dramatic location emerge from the words spoken. The Theatre of Dionysus is not a naturalistic space, and freed of nineteenth-century naturalistic assumptions, the flexibility of the Athenian space emerges. So when the setting does change (as in *Eumenides* and Sophocles' *Ajax*) there are clear means to mark how that is accomplished, including the departure of the chorus, which does not happen here. This use of the verb 'refocus' in scholarly discussions obscures the need for a specific staging decision. If it is felt that the 10 metres or so between the tomb and the door is not a realistic distance between these two locations, I would agree; but distances need not be realistic. Action has been concentrated on the centre of the *orchēstra* for the first half of the play, and then shifts to the *skēnē* door for the second half. The placement of actors on stage may cause a spectator to refocus, but it does not come at the expense of consistent stage space.

The connection between the two locations has been defined by Electra's movements. Within the dramatic narrative, she arrives from the palace and returns there. As we saw (Chapter 2.1), Scullion argued she arrives (with the chorus) through the central door at line 16, and returns there at 584, as she is instructed to do (579–80).[43] Electra travels from the tomb to the palace door retracing her earlier steps from *thymelē* to door, in plain view. She leaves Orestes and Pylades at the tomb for the stasimon. Then Orestes walks from the tomb to the door, replicating the journey made by his father in Agamemnon. Where Agamemnon left his silent companion Cassandra, Orestes, entering in secret, can approach with Pylades. The continued presence of the chorus knits the two locations together as the young men approach the door.

This then becomes another of Taplin's 'mirror scenes', where the action echoes a previously staged event: 'the Greek tragedians often set up pairs of scenes, and almost invariably set up the similarities in order to bring out the differences'.[44] In this case, the appearance of a male character (almost certainly played by the same actor) replicates the basic physical action of the previous play – enter and proceed to *thymelē* (*Ag.* 783, *LB* 1); move to central door (*Ag.* 958, *LB* 652) – while still allowing enough variation for the audience to compare and contrast the two approaches: victim/avenger; unaware/aware, royal entrance/secret entrance; with Cassandra/with Pylades. Increasing the variation further (removing the precise visual echo in the movement, for example) risks diminishing the apparent parallelism. Agamemnon's tomb maps onto the location where his chariot had stopped in *Agamemnon*, and corresponds to the audience focal point at or near the *thymelē*.[45] Once the action shifts to the palace, the *thymelē* is not used, but it remains in the visual field for the spectators. The chorus, having made libations at the grave, have left their vases in and around the altar/tomb. As a result, the *thymelē* looks like an actual Greek tomb (Chapter 2.2). Garlanded, decorated, this image persists even as the dramatic action has moved to the palace, and the visual symbol of the offerings (represented by the now-empty vases the chorus have left there) provides a constant symbolic reminder of the false gift from Clytaemestra, and the massive and impressive song that had affirmed the choice Orestes had made to kill his mother. The *choes* remain crucial, because they demonstrate that the grave does not remain unmarked for the spectator, disappearing into the background: the continued presence of props actively deny that the play has refocused its setting. The grave remains in the visual field, not in a spatial relationship with the events transpiring at the palace door, but in a conceptual one, deepening Orestes' ongoing ties with his father.

3.4 On the Threshold

Orestes and Pylades approach the palace door and knock: 'Boy! Boy!' Orestes calls as he kicks the door (653), employing the standard Athenian way of making one's presence known inside a house. This becomes a familiar scene in comedy, with the same cry heard in the door-knockings in Aristophanes at *Acharnians* 395, *Birds* 57, and *Frogs* 37. It is not a scene that recurs in tragedy, however: there is a (humorous) door-knocking at Euripides, *Helen* 437, without the call for the household slave. Based on this later evidence, the tone of the motif here is suspect.[46] It is undoubtedly quotidian, reflecting the everyday rather than the elevated grandeur or dignity naturally associated with tragedy. This establishes a tone that maintains the contrast with the approach in *Agamemnon*, where Clytaemestra had delivered 17 stately lines to accompany the slow procession to the palace (*Ag.* 958–74).

In *Libation Bearers* it is the door-knocking that is drawn out, with Orestes knocking three times before he receives an answer, the Doorkeeper's single line (657). Does the door crack open and a head poke out to speak? Is it a voice from within the house, with the speaker remaining unseen? Whatever the staging decision, Orestes' access to the house is blocked not by Clytaemestra, who had dominated control of the threshold in *Agamemnon*, but by an unnamed slave.[47] Orestes' request for Aegisthus, 'if he's receptive to strangers [*philoxen*']' (656), is met with a colloquial and gruff response (657 'Yeah, yeah, I hear you. Where is the stranger [*ho xenos*] from? Where?'). *Xenia*, evoked in both of these lines, is the guest-host relationship, where a *xenos* can be a guest or a stranger (who deserves hospitality) or a foreigner (who is likely to need hospitality), or even the host: the whole network of relationship presumes a rapport under the protection of Zeus. The irony continues as Orestes asks for any of those in power within, suggesting that it might be a woman (658, 664). His preference is clear: men speak directly, but with women speech is restrained (665–7, with 665 *aidōs*, modesty or bashfulness, being a singularly inappropriate barrier to be felt by the Clytaemestra of *Agamemnon*).

Then she is there, again at the threshold, Clytaemestra controlling access to the house, as twilight draws near, literally and symbolically (660–2).[48] Despite her nightmare the previous evening, she is an instant and gracious host, inviting the strangers (667 *xenoi*) inside for a bath and a comfortable bed. The mention of 'hot baths' (670) must recall the appearance of Agamemnon's corpse at *Ag.* 1372 in a silver bathtub.[49] She is attended (either by an extra adopting the role of the Doorkeeper, who may have been visible earlier, or by another palace slave; the practical difference between these is almost nothing), and it is to her attendant that she gives the order to receive the guests (712–15). The opening of the house to the strangers symbolizes the effectiveness of the deception almost before it has begun. In a naturalistic theatre, one would expect Clytaemestra to be wearing a different costume than in *Agamemnon*, and perhaps to be wearing a different mask. The play does not say how the queen appears, but we must assume she is instantly recognizable. I presume that the actor wears the same mask as in *Agamemnon*: though seven years have passed, Clytaemestra is still a mature woman and in her prime. A different costume for this play – one not stained with blood! – is more likely: instant identification from the audience is nonetheless necessary before she begins to speak.

Orestes presents himself as a Phocian stranger who after a chance meeting with Strophius has learned that Orestes is dead (682). The

embedded direct speech from Strophius (680–7) lends verisimilitude
to the account, but it also casts thoughts about Orestes' proper place
in terms of the treatment of his imagined corpse: will he remain a
xenos, living abroad forever as a metic (684 *metoikon* is a distinctly
Athenian word for 'resident alien'), or will he return home as a *philos*
(friend and family, not the *xenos* he now appears to be)? Orestes
provides pathos as he subtly elevates his own reputation: 'sides of
a bronze urn now conceal the ashes of the nobly mourned man'
(686–7), so that the final words of the fictional speech covertly praise
the inventor. There is no bronze urn to be seen: that is a detail added
in Sophocles' *Electra*. Orestes dissembles, claiming not to know if he
addresses kin or not, as his speech concludes.

What is the reaction to the news Orestes is dead? The details of
the response (691–9) will be considered in the next section, but the
profound grief expressed is unexpected. Following the speech, the
play returns to the polite conversation between *xenoi*: guest and host
meet each other, but the host is unaware that the guest is her son.
Eleven of the 22 uses of the *xen-* root within the play are in this short
scene, as Aeschylus emphasizes the estrangement between the two
(in comparison, only six of the play's forty-three uses of the *phil-* root
are here).[50] Throughout, spectators interpret Clytaemestra's reaction
in the light of what they know from *Agamemnon*. Her tone, in the
offer of *xenia* and a bath above all, is therefore always suspect. Both
she and Orestes are employing irony that will excite spectators. Is this
the public face of Clytaemestra, or is she genuinely a changed woman,
having been humbled by her nightmare? The audience simply does
not know, and it is not clear there is a particular literary precedent
that might be shaping expectations: not every spectator will know
Stesichorus in any case, even presuming Clytaemestra's response
when faced with Orestes was unambiguous there. My sense is that
an audience works to build continuity between Clytaemestra here
and the last time it saw her in *Agamemnon*, and that consequently

it understands everything she says here as deliberately duplicitous. Those thinking along these lines read extra meaning into the implied threats of her servant at 715, for example. At the same time, Orestes is accepting *xenia* with the intention of murdering his hosts, and the violation that this entails is also meant to be shocking, and perhaps even offensive. Both speakers know more than they are telling the other, and the audience, with a perspective of even more superior knowledge, can appreciate their gambits, even as it sees Orestes successfully dupe his mother. Pylades and Orestes enter the palace, leaving the chorus alone on stage for the first time in the play.

A final issue to be discussed in this scene concerns Orestes' attendants: the manuscripts preserve three plurals in the phrase 'and these fellow travellers walking behind' (713). This line is the only indication that Pylades and Orestes might be accompanied by anyone else, and it changes the understanding of the stage picture significantly. It also stands at odds with the most straightforward meaning of 675 where Orestes claimed he was carrying his own belongings. Pauw emended the text at 713 so the plurals become singular, and therefore referred only to Pylades, and that is a reasonable correction. One nevertheless wonders how the passage might have first been corrupted. Taplin suggests that this:

> can hardly be a scribal error; it is surely a deliberate alteration. Only one motive seems likely: that a later producer wanted to introduce extra mute stage-figures. A group of travellers, all equipped with hats and packs, would provide a picturesque and crowded spectacle. … If this train of argument is right, then this is an intriguing and instructive glimpse of the work of later producers. Aeschylus was too bare for their taste; and they took an easy opportunity to introduce more colour and spectacle.[51]

We have seen that the *Oresteia* was reperformed in the 420s, and subsequent reperformances into the fourth century are probable (Chapters 2.2 and 2.4). With each of these later performances, different production decisions would be possible.[52] Both possibilities work thematically: since the implicit point of comparison is the grand entrance of Agamemnon, Orestes and Pylades arrive humbly, either in a group (and therefore similarly) or alone (and therefore different). The matter is made more suspicious by the fact that the manuscript M initially omitted lines 712–14 in its transcription, and they were subsequently written in the margin. Most likely, they were skipped in the copying process (both 711 and 714 end with the word *prosphora*, and the copyist's eye would have skipped past one to the other). In any case, these instructions are the only clear indication to Orestes' entourage, which may be an indirect record of the play's performance history after the initial performance in 458.

3.5 Electra

The disappearance of Electra at 584, with no further appearance or even mention in the play, is striking: 'This uncompromising abandonment of a named character is remarkable ... She has played her part, and so she is dispensed with'.[53] The audience has seen Electra's emotional transformation, from the unhappy daughter enjoined to make offerings on her mother's behalf, to the delighted sister reunited with her absent brother, who turns out to be the avenger she had also sought. She helps galvanize Orestes through the *kommos*, and then goes into the house to provide whatever assistance might be needed (579–80). Then she is gone. For subsequent fifth-century tragedians, Electra became the emotional focus of this tragic narrative, but in *Libation Bearers*, she is simply abandoned. Or so it appears.

When Orestes delivers the false news of his own death, the immediate response is one of utter bereavement:

> Ah me, we are completely, utterly ruined! Curse of this house, so hard
> to wrestle free of, how much you keep your eye on, even when it's

placed well out of the way! Scoring hits at long range with well-aimed arrows, you strip me, wretched me, of my loved ones [*philōn*]! And now Orestes—he was showing wisdom in keeping his feet clear of the deadly mire; but now the hope [*elpis*] there was in the house of a cure [*iatros*] for your evil revelry—write it down as having betrayed us! (*LB* 691–9, tr. Sommerstein)

After the opening image of being utterly destroyed (literally, the Greek of 691 says 'Ah me, we are completely sacked [like a city], from top to bottom'), the speaker calls upon a personified Curse (*Ara*), which has stripped the speaker of *philoi* (695), and names Orestes as a hoped-for doctor or cure (699 *iatros*) for the ills of the house. As a response from Clytaemestra, to whom the speech is assigned in most translations, this represents a completely unguarded, and unexpected, sympathetic response. It becomes a momentary sign of her vulnerability. The audience seemingly has an immediate sense of maternal grief, anticipating the appeal to her breast when she next confronts Orestes at sword-point, but which is quickly covered by concerns over the practicalities of receiving guests. Alternately, this appearance of grief may be feigned – it is the sort of response a bereaved mother should provide – and the hollowness of her words is demonstrated by the speed with which she changes to issues of hospitality for the messengers (compare her hollow reception of her husband at *Ag.* 855–913). It is not clear which of these psychological explanations is to be preferred, and while an actor's delivery could work to remove audience doubt, such an ambiguity is not easily paralleled in the psychology of fifth-century tragic characters.[54] Later, the nurse Cilissa will indicate her belief that Clytaemestra is dissembling (*LB* 737–39). Orestes, feigning to be a dispassionate messenger, says he wishes his news were more favourable. Having recovered her composure, Clytaemestra's next speech is dispassionate, offering hospitality (710 *xenous*) as the news is conveyed to Aegisthus (708–18): indeed, she 'seems (despite her protestations of grief) quite

eager for Aigisthos, the master of the house, to hear it as well.'[55] This
is the queen again in control of herself, confident of her position. She
even insists, 'we are not short of friends' (717 *kou spanizontes philōn*).
Clytaemestra then leads Orestes and Pylades into the palace.

It is worth considering an alternative assignment of *LB* 691–9. A
few scholars have argued that Electra in fact delivered the speech, who
would have returned with Clytaemestra and her attendants at 668.[56]
Electra, of course, knows the identity of Orestes, and so her emotional
outburst is not a sudden revelation of unanticipated feelings, but is
instead calculated to add verisimilitude to Orestes' account. There
are no palaeographical reasons against the assignment, and as the
only speech from Electra in the scene it would appear as a clever
fulfillment of the instructions Orestes had given her at 579–80. The
theory is attractive, and deserves more consideration than it is often
given. It removes the inconsistency of friends (none here at 695 but
plenty for Clytaemestra at 717): that Electra has no friends and looks
to Orestes at an *iatros* is straightforward, and frames her hope in terms
of Apollo (who is also latent in the arrows fired from a distance at
694); in the mouth of Clytaemestra, the claim appears inconsistent. It
is similarly unclear what Clytaemestra would see as the illness needing
an *iatros*. Evil bacchic revelry in the house (698) is most naturally
tied to Clytemaestra's wrongful usurpation of the throne, and similar
language has been used with reference to the Erinyes (*Ag.* 1188–90).
All of this imagery more naturally fits Electra's character, as Seaford
argues.[57] There would also be no doubt about Electra's psychology at
this point, which is consistent and explicable: she is following instructions effectively. This assignment also deepens the irony: though
Electra believes that what she says is not true (she thinks one thing
and says another), the play will show that her false words are fulfilled:
Orestes will be struck down from afar; he is not a remedy for the
house's ills; and Electra will indeed be stripped of her *philoi*.

In terms of characterization, both possibilities introduce new depth to the character speaking. Clytaemestra had been a dominating and impenetrable force throughout *Agamemnon*. *Libation Bearers* has shown her still in control, but with cracks in that dominance, as she is afflicted by night terrors and seeks to appease the ghost of the man she murdered. The audience has been shown that there is an exploitable weakness for the avengers. This speech would show Clytaemestra retaining her power, and able to recapture the voice of authority, even as she brings her would-be killers under her roof, unaware that she has been duped. Assigned to her, this speech is the indication of her weakness. Electra, in contrast, is strengthened as a character if she delivers these lines. The last time she had spoken was her final prayer at 508–9; she had stood silently until she entered the palace at 584, and had remained silent on her return at 668–90, unmentioned, standing among the attendants, not unlike her initial entry with the chorus of servants. For her, lines 691–9 show Electra to be as an independent thinker, capable of deception and again demonstrating her essential contribution to the revenge narrative. Either possibility could be right.

The decision to whom the lines are given additionally has implications for the role division in the play, for if this is Electra speaking, then the same actor cannot play both Electra and Clytaemestra. Such a doubling is attractive: two characters connected by blood would share the same physical body and voice but whose personalities and motivations are so completely at odds. This pairing has been generally adopted, which, factoring in the concerns raised in chapter 1.3, leads to the following division of speaking roles for the play:[58]

Actor A: Orestes, Cilissa, Aegisthus
Actor B: Servant, Pylades
Actor C: Electra, Doorkeeper, Clytaemestra

We do not know which of these roles Aeschylus himself played. This is the division I have argued for previously, assigning Aegisthus to actor

A in order to maintain he casting of the role in *Agamemnon*; Cilissa could in fact be played by any of the three.[59] Now, I am less certain. If Electra speaks *LB* 691–9, then a different assignment of roles is needed:

Actor A:	Orestes, Cilissa, Aegisthus
Actor B:	Electra, Servant, Pylades
Actor C:	Doorkeeper, Clytaemestra

With this casting, actor C does not appear until line 668, a delayed entry that could be theatrically effective after Clytaemestra's dominating presence in *Agamemnon*. Again Cilissa could be played by any of the actors: if it is actor A, the nurse's connection with her fosterling would be reinforced as the Orestes actor adopts another character to describe Orestes' infancy.[60] My inclination is to keep the role with actor A, because of the structural parallels between the Cilissa and Aegisthus scenes, discussed in Chapter 4.2. With this assignment of parts, and the other stage directions suggested in this book, no actor is required to make a backstage move: they always change masks and return at the last entrance to the performance space that they had used.

There are additional consequences for this second division of parts, which the former allocation did not generate. Actor B has been onstage with Orestes as Electra since the *parodos*, which means that the performer who silently accompanies Orestes throughout the play as Pylades is played by an unspeaking extra until *LB* 718 (unlike speaking performers, there seems to have been no limit on the number of extras available, as long as the *chorēgos* paid whatever expenses were needed). The scene at *LB* 668–718 would show all three speaking actors together (in the roles of Orestes, Electra and Clyaemestra) with Pylades being played by an extra. This would, I feel, enhance the surprise felt when Pylades does eventually speak at *LB* 900–2: in the confusion of entrances and exits (see Chapter 4.4), the substitution of actor B in the mask of Pylades would constitute a greater surprise.[61] The audience knows from *Agamemnon* that

Aeschylus has three actors available, and I now feel the surprise of Pylades speaking would be enhanced by this assignment of roles. The later tradition (Euripides, *Electra* 1249, *Iphigenia among the Taurians* 695–6, 915, *Orestes* 1078–80, 1658–59) that Pylades marries Electra may also be reflected in the light of this casting.[62] Further, since actor B is associated with the 'voice of Apollo' throughout the tetralogy (playing Cassandra, Pylades, Pythia and Apollo), it is legitimate to assume that some in the audience will now see Electra in this light as well, as an agent of the god actively facilitating Orestes' mission of revenge. The Apollonine features of *LB* 691–9 (the reference to arrows shot from a great distance at 694 and the use of *iatros* in 699) would reinforce this association. Note however that this casting choice does not depend on the assignment of 691–9: pairing Electra with Pylades makes sense in any case, even if *Electra* does not return at 668,[63] and this seems to me to be the most probable assignment of roles.

The first appearance of Clyaemestra in this play has been carefully anticipated and in this short episode (*LB* 653–718), the audience sees her unwittingly invite her killer into the palace under the protection of her hospitality, all while thinking she remains steadfastly in control of the house. Except for the one-line from the Doorkeeper at 657, the episode consists of six speeches, which comprise three pairs:

i.	Orestes	653–67	announcing his arrival
ii.	Clytaemestra	668–73	receiving *xenoi*
iii.	Orestes	674–90	announcing the supposed death of Orestes
iv.	Electra (?)	691–9	grieving at the news, lacking *philoi*
v.	Orestes	700–6	stressing the importance of *xenia* and *philia*
vi.	Clytaemestra	707–18	claiming to have *philoi*, and offering *xenia*

The tight alternation establishes a rhythm that leads to the fatal decision by the queen. Agamemnon's entry had been stately and momentous, and he was duped. In *Libation Bearers*, the tables have turned and his avenger enters in a lowly disguise.

Matricide and Madness

The last third of *Libation Bearers* presents a whirlwind of activity that is meant to be dizzying to a spectator. These short staccato scenes suggest frantic movement, and this heightens the feeling of intense action, especially when compared to the slower pace of *Agamemnon* and the first movements of this play. With Orestes having gained access to the palace, the chorus is left alone onstage for the first time. The short anapestic passage (719–29) recognizes the presence of Agamemnon's tomb (722–4) and the chthonic powers that drive Orestes' revenge, which include the god Hermes (722 *Chthōn*, 727 *chthonion d' Hermēn*). Possibly, the *koryphaios* continues to deliver the anapestic lines as in the *kommos*, but more likely this is the entire chorus chanting together (as subsequently at 855–68). As a result, there is a shift to just a single voice when the music stops and the *koryphaios* announces the appearance of Cilissa, the nurse.

4.1 Cilissa

The appearance at the door of Orestes' childhood wet-nurse is a surprise. The short episode (*LB* 730–82) of dialogue between the nurse and the *koryphaios* is seemingly incidental to Orestes' revenge action, but the intimate details that it provides means that spectators cannot accept the maternal connection implied in Clytaemestra's dream unquestioningly. Cilissa makes the situation messier. Further, within the scene the *koryphaios* changes the action of the plot in a way that ensures Orestes' eventual success. The *koryphaios'* opening is addressed to a fellow slave: she observes that the woman, Orestes' former nurse, is weeping, and gives her name, Cilissa (732). The name is a demonym, identifying her place of origin as Cilicia, in the southeast of modern-day Turkey, just north of Cyprus.

To begin, Cilissa presents herself as any domestic servant being sent on a mission for her master. Ordinary servants are common in tragedy, and as she begins (*LB* 734–43), she outlines her mission to summon Aegisthus. What is unexpected is that the slave woman reveals her personal thoughts about Clytaemestra's mental disposition. In fact, she is explicit about the queen's duplicity: 'before the household slaves, she adopted a sullen expression, hiding the laughter within' (737–9). So saying, Cilissa divides the feelings of the household from those of its mistress, recognizing the wrongness of the present situation. Though a slave, she, like the chorus, identifies with Agamemnon, and, importantly, she knows the disposition of the *koryphaios* already. There is resistance to Clytaemestra and Aegisthus, and here we see it expressed in confidence. This in turn reveals some information about how the actor playing Clytaemestra responded to the news in the previous scene: presumably, Cilissa is adding information that was not otherwise available to the audience, which means that in some sense the actor was playing it 'straight'. Clytaemestra is not a cartoonish villain, but has been humanized and made comprehensible. Spectators are unlikely to question the veracity of Cilissa's observation, since it represents unexpected evidence to which they would not expect to have access.

Cilissa then pauses in her mission to reminisce about the baby Orestes (743–65). While still using the language and metre of tragedy, Cilissa introduces ordinary everyday details into her speech, as her words assume qualities that are non-regal, non-elite and non-mythic. There was an element of this in *Agamemnon* as well, when the Herald describes the poor living conditions at Troy, with poor bedding, damp tents, and lice (*Ag.* 556–62), but the present scene builds on the apparent incongruity of conflicting registers. Cilissa describes the greatest challenges (745 'pains') she has experienced within the household, which apparently concern the rearing of baby Orestes. Given the history of murder and bloodshed within the house, this bathetic substitution is surprising. She describes how the house's greatest woes were caused by 'dear Orestes, the object of my soul's concern, whom I raised [*exethrepsa*] having received him from his mother' (749–50). The details that follow add to the charming and unexpected humour of the situation (755–60):

> For a child still in swaddling cannot speak at all
> if it is hungry, or thirsty, or needs to pee,
> and the young bowels of children act on their own.
> I was a prophetess [*promantis*] of these things: I suppose I was often
> mistaken, a launderer of the child's swaddling.
> A cleaner and nurse hold the same job.

It is the news of Orestes' death that has actually caused Cilissa grief (761–3), but that is not immediately clear as she speaks, and the protracted discussion, introducing details that are not ordinarily associated with tragedy, mark the importance of the scene.

Cilissa's reminiscence challenges the audience's understanding of Clytaemestra. The queen's dream had presented her as nursing a serpent, who was identified with Orestes. Here, Orestes is compared to a speechless beast (753 *boton*) nursed by a slave (731 *trophon*, 754 *trephein, trophou*). While it is possible that both women nursed Orestes, the introduction of these details now, in a context which points to Clytaemestra's duplicity, forces spectators to re-assess their interpretation of the reported dream. Aeschylus does not need to introduce this character, and his choice to do so destabilizes any assessment of the queen that has been made. There is also a weird echo of Apollo, whose prophecies were implicitly questioned earlier (*LB* 559). The scene also evokes the description of another nurse, Eurycleia, who likewise received Odysseus when he was first born (*Odyssey* 19.353–55).[1] The profound connection between Eurycleia and Odysseus serves as a literary paradigm for Cilissa and Orestes, and the comparison, given the earthiness of the presentation of Cilissa, may not reinforce Orestes' heroism. The syntax in lines 751–3 is impossible to construe, and likely points to a lacuna in the text: the lost passage may be a single line, but could perhaps be more. Cilissa's allegiance to Agamemnon is emphasized when she claims she nursed Orestes 'for his father' (762 *patri*; Agamemnon has apparently not been mentioned in the scene so far), and so this is another unexpected detail, as she proceeds to leave on her errand to fetch Aegisthus.

The *koryphaios* then enters into irregular *stichomythia* with Cilissa (766–82), asking the precise details of her message, which is that Clytaemestra 'tells him to bring his spear-carrying attendants' (769). The *koryphaios* changes that instruction, urging her to fetch Aegisthus but for him to come unattended (770–3). There is no clear parallel of slaves deliberately disobeying their masters' orders in Greek tragedy: the closest comparison comes almost fifty years later, when the *koryphaios* physically blocks another character's movements at Euripides' *Helen* 1627–41 (412 BCE).[2] Cilissa does not know the truth that Orestes is actually alive (the *koryphaios* does not reveal everything that she knows, 776–8). In that respect, she is in the position of Electra in Sophocles' play, looking at the empty urn that she believes holds her brother's ashes. Though Cilissa does not know the truth, she acquiesces to substitute the *koryphaios'* instructions for those of Clytaemestra, with a simplistic hope that the gods will help make all things right.

There is no comparable scene between slaves in Greek tragedy.

Aeschylus' choice to introduce the nurse at all raises questions about the meaning of Clytaemestra's dream that had underpinned much of the play's action so far. It uses the audience's expectations of breastfeeding and wet-nursing to consider what constitutes acceptable maternal care, drawing on both practical knowledge (fifth-century Athenian mothers typically nursed their own young if they could) and mythological precedent (drawing primarily on Homer). Aeschylus' choice to characterize Cilissa as he has seems to upsets the fundamentally serious tone of the tragedy (see also Chapter 4.6). In real life, slave women would be silenced: theirs is a suppressed voice, one that combines the concerns of child care with criticism of her mistress. Finally, by having Cilissa swayed by the *koryphaios*, the chorus changes the action of the plot and provides a crucial step in Orestes' eventual success.

4.2 Stasimon and Structure

There is an architecture within *Libation Bearers* that emerges following the *kommos*, by which the stasimon at 783–837 becomes a turning-point or lynchpin for the plot. Following this choral song, the action of the play accelerates, but through a technique of ring-composition, there is a feeling of repeated closure as each piece seems to follow naturally on the last. Ring-composition is an oral technique found in Homer and which is used to frame a narrative. It is not typically used on the grand scale seen in *Libation Bearers*, but in this section I hope to demonstrate both its relevance to the play as an organizational technique and the opportunity it provides for theatrical surprise. The rings run six layers deep (A, B, C, D, E, F) before they begin to work themselves outwards (E′, D′, C′, B′, A′). The effect foregrounds the central unit, in this case the choral stasimon, granting it an unusual prominence. Each of the other paired units, however, resonates though the correspondence. Table 3 provides a structural overview of the play, identifying the units. While the normal alteration of stasima and iambic scenes creates a regular rhythm of alternating sung and spoken within a tragedy naturally, this degree of correspondence is unusual, and requires a conscious crafting by the playwright.

At the start of the play, Orestes' *nostos* led to the recognition with Electra for which she had waited so long. Its narrative development was essentially linear, bringing together the two siblings (in the presence of the chorus and Pylades), which allowed them to unite in the invocation of the spirit of Agamemnon in the *kommos*, which itself was a wonder of poetic architecture. Following the recognition, the action of revenge can begin. The correspondences to be seen operate on both thematic and performative levels. The sung portions of the revenge-section of the play are the cues to the audience to make the associations. The five choral units (B, D, F, D′, B′) create a pattern: stasimon, anapests, stasimon, anapests, stasimon. The use of anapestic passages (D, D′) as act-dividing songs is noticable, and the contrast between them illuminating for the theological dimension of Orestes' act, as the D unit connects Orestes with chthonic forces; the D′ unit with Zeus. In both of these, the chorus is left alone on stage but strophic singing is not begun. Similarly, the two framing choral songs invite the spectator to measure them against one another, as B uses mythological paradigms to explore Clytaemestra's guilt, and B′ insists on the righteousness of Orestes' revenge, maintaining the Olympian emphasis (see Chapter 4.4). These are elements also found in the central unit (F), discussed below.

These choral correspondences are not in themselves enough to prove the case for meaningful ring-composition. The iambic portions too must resonate, as they do, creating meaningful connections to the scene to which each corresponds. This is most easily seen in the way the short Aegisthus episode resonates with Cilissa (E, E′). A powerful male contrasted with a female slave (both possibly played by the

Table 3 Structural outline of *Libation Bearers*

1–21	Orestes and Pylades			
22–83	Chorus (strophic *parodos*)			
84–151	Electra and Chorus			
152–63	Chorus (astrophic)			
164–211	Electra and Chorus			
212–305	Electra, Orestes, Pylades, and Chorus			RECOGNITION
306-478	**Great *Kommos***			
479–584	Orestes and Electra	A		
585–652	Stasimon	B		
653–718	**Clytaemestra**	C		
719–29	anapaests	D		
730–82	Cilissa	E		
783–837	**Stasimon**	F		
838–54	Aigisthus	E′		
855–74	anapaests	D′		
875–930	**Clytaemestra**	C′		
931–72	Stasimon	B′		
973–1076	Orestes and Pylades	A′		REVENGE

same actor) creates an interesting contrast in what are two of the shortest 'episodes' in extant Greek tragedy. Cilissa had gone in search of Aegisthus, and had been urged by the chorus to have him return unaccompanied: the success of that mission is apparent, reinforced by the structural pairing, and shows the audience that the tables have turned. This is the first 'echo' a spectator will perceive, to be followed immediately by anapests which constitute a second echo, the working outward of the narrative pattern's concentric rings.

The two scenes with Clytaemestra (C, C′) also invite direct associations with each other, as each documents a vital moment in the play's narrative development. The first scene in this pair represents the duping of the queen, where she asserts control, but is overcome by Orestes' cunning. The pairing of this scene with her second appearance, as she now knows who Orestes is and makes her desperate appeal to her maternal breast, is therefore coloured both by hints of deception (echoing the cunning *dolos* by which Orestes crossed the threshold Clytaemestra had so zealously guarded in *Agamemnon*) and the continued progress of the revenge action. Both scenes also involve a minor domestic slave, the Doorkeeper and the Servant, further reinforcing the correspondence. It is possible, then, that the crucial and unexpected speech by Pylades at *LB* 900–2 is anticipated in the unexpected cry of Electra at *LB* 691–8, if she delivers that speech (see Chapter 3.5). This degree of correspondence is not necessary, but when it occurs audience members may perceive an unfolding pattern, which allows some narrative anticipation. There is an inherent rightness when Pylades does eventually speak, even if it comes as a surprise.

The outer frame (A, A′) also provides a series of meaningful echoes. In the initial scene after the *kommos*, Orestes and Electra beseech the spirit of Agamemnon to support their coming revenge, and the supernatural working of Clytaemestra's dream becomes apparent. The play's final scene, Orestes and Pylades stand over the bodies of Clytaemestra and Aegisthus, having accomplished their revenge, and the supernatural working of Clytaemestra's Erinyes becomes apparent. These scenes frame the revenge action, but the chthonic workings shift significantly, meaning that the vulnerability of Clytaemestra exposed in the description of the dream will be answered by Orestes' vulnerability when confronted with the Erinyes.

Central to this narrative pattern in the revenge action is the stasimon at *LB* 783–837 (F), which is given an emphatic prominence. Its strophic structure is straightforward but unusual, as Aeschylus employs a unique mesode to interrupt each strophic pair (returning to Greek letters now: A, mes. α, A′, B, mes. β, B′, Γ, mes. γ, Γ′). The choral lyric is also woefully corrupt, having suffered extensive damage early in the tradition (this is seen because the scholia recognize the damaged text). It is therefore rash to press any interpretation too far, but it is possible to perceive the song's overall trajectory, which again highlights the theological frame within which *Libation Bearers* operates.

The first triad (783–99) is addressed directly to Zeus, in the name of justice (787 *dikas*), with the antistrophe developing an elaborate metaphor in which Orestes is now a young colt pulling a chariot of revenge, hurtling headlong in a race. As Garvie describes, the yoke image was prominent in *Agamemnon*, applied to Agamemnon, Odysseus, Cassandra, the chorus, and the city of Troy. Here that imagery is passed onto a second generation, across plays of the tetralogy.[3] Orestes is apparently yoked alone (or with an implied Electra? Pylades?), but the image of athletic ambition is resonant. Why is Orestes associated with an orphaned colt? Orestes isn't an orphan exactly (yet?), and Cilissa has just embodied a substitute maternal figure, which makes the image here more inapt. An orphan should be nuzzling for milk (like the serpent in Clytaemestra's dream?), or would be given to another mare to nurse, with Cilissa implicitly assuming that function. Whatever the meaning, it is yoked to a chariot of death, ruin, or vengeance, with a steady beat rhythmically matched by the choral song.

The second triad (800–18) invokes three divinities, but their identities are less certain. Easiest is the 'child of Maia' (813) in the *antistrophē*, Hermes, a constant presence beside Orestes throughout the play and a god who represents cunning action (*dolos*) and who crosses between Olympian and chthonic spaces. Before this, in the mesode, is a god of a 'mouth' (808) or opening, and so likely Apollo at Delphi (though the image also evokes the doorway of the *skēnē* visible onstage). Most uncertain are the 'like-minded gods' (802) in the *strophē*, within the house who tend the storeroom. Since the Greeks do not have an easy equivalent of the Roman Penates (storehouse gods), this might refer to Hestia, or Zeus Ktesios (an aspect of Zeus associated with possessions), but neither of these has a place elsewhere in the extant trilogy. More likely is that Erinyes are meant, spirits of revenge that operate within the house.[4] As discussed in Chapter 2.3, every mention of the Furies so far in the play has been to Agamemnon's Erinyes, not those of Clytaemestra. These are the gods within that are like-minded with the avengers and are supported by *Dikē*. Though the reference to them is indirect, the mental effort to interpret the reference is a distraction from the real threat that is imminent from Clytaemestra's Erinyes. All three of the powers identified in this triad are therefore liminal, representing the intersection of Olympian and chthonic within the darkness of an enclosed space.

The third triad (819–37) disperses the prayerful energies in three directions. In the *strophē*, the chorus anticipates its victory song as if carried on a successful sailing wind. The mesode is directed to Orestes personally, though he is within the palace, urging him to insist that he is his father's child, and not that of his mother when she beseeches him. This curiously anticipates Clytaemestra's appeal to her breast, yet to come, as well as the resolution of his trial in *Eumenides*. The chorus see the coming victory as their victory: though slaves, they are fully aligned with the values of the previous ruler, and not with their present circumstances. Restoration, though revenge, is within reach, and so they give vicarious advice to the child that they've not seen before. The strength of the chorus, their self-possession as slave women, contrasts with the vacillation and weakness expressed by the chorus of *Agamemnon* when these performers were elders of Argos. Finally, the *antistrophē* introduces a new mythological paradigm, of Perseus decapitating the gorgon Medusa. The example of Perseus instantly characterizes Clytaemestra as a monster to be slain. That's almost too easy, though, and denies the depths in her that the tetralogy has been seeking to establish. There are two further similarities that can be teased out of the association, though. First, Orestes, like Perseus, is approaching secretly, with cunning.[5] Second, Orestes, like Perseus, is guided by Hermes. Hermes' appropriateness for Orestes works on a few levels: Orestes is a traveller, he has brought a message, he is employing *dolos*, and he is, with the gods' help, building links between the living and the dead. All of these fall under the purview of Hermes, and the constant presence of Pylades perhaps reflects an earlier tradition in which Orestes is accompanied by Hermes on his journey.

Even without textual difficulties, the unusual form of this ode and its vivid if obscure imagery challenges the listener to fill in apparent blanks. The parts of the ode can be reassembled, yielding deeper meanings. Each *strophē* builds a sequence tracing Orestes' revenge, from Zeus and Justice (A), to Agamemnon's Erinyes (B), to the ship image representing the chorus' victory (Γ). The three mesodes, when strophic responsion is held in abeyance, invoke Zeus (mes. α), Apollo (mes. β), and then speak to the absent Orestes directly (mes. γ). Finally, each *antistrophē* presents a powerful associated image for Orestes' revenge: an orphaned colt (A′), Hermes as an encourager (B′), and finally Perseus (Γ'). The confused jumble of images here is all appropriate, but not fully able to be disentangled. They are threads to be drawn out differently in this foregrounded song that lead directly into the performance of the revenge.

4.3 Aegisthus

Aegisthus the effeminate adulterer enters, and, in the shortest scene in an extant tragedy (*LB* 838–54; only 17 lines), identifies himself and enters into the palace unawares.[6] Short scenes like this are found in the comedy of Aristophanes, but are unexpected in tragedy. Aegisthus' eagerness to go to his death grants an irony to his haste. He is worse at hiding his feelings than Clytaemestra, and, following the instructions of Cilissa as suggested by the *koryphaios*, he has arrived unaccompanied. The inversion of the Cilissa scene is already evident, but is magnified by the short conversation he has with the *koryphaios*. Aegisthus' concern is to learn for certain the fate of Orestes. Word of Orestes' death has come to him at third hand, and there is a blurring of the messengers. He learned the news from Cilissa, and so the message comes 'from a messenger' (838 *hupangelos*, cf. 773), and the *koryphaios* slyly disparages the trustworthiness of messengers generally (849 *angelōn*); as a result, Aegisthus wants to interrogate the supposed Phocian, who is also a messenger (851 *ton angelon*, 709, 773). It is not quite the case that the reference to messengers is necessarily metatheatrical when used in the context of a tragedy (though it does become that when Euripides has Electra ask at *Electra* 759, 'Where are the messengers?'). The repetition here, in light of what the audience knows, is self-conscious. Where Cilissa introduced charming bathetic details, Aegisthus lives in a world of hyperbole, in which the wounds of the house continue to fester from the murder of Agamemnon (841–3). This would be acceptable from Electra or Orestes, but is an unusually vivid description of the home he has occupied as regent for the past seven years. Aegisthus' exit line, 'He [the Phocian stranger] will certainly not fool a mind with its eyes open' (*LB* 854), is delicious in its short-sightedness. Then he is gone, again leaving the chorus alone onstage.

A short passage of anapests (855–68, answering those at 719–30) follows. The chorus telegraphs the coming murders in its prayer to Zeus. Orestes' name is postponed until 867, amidst a wrestling metaphor, at which point a voice cries out from behind the *skēnē*: *e e ototoi* (869). Aegisthus' death-cry again fulfills the wish of the Watchman in the prologue to *Agamemnon*, who had prayed that the house could take voice (*Ag.* 34–5). When Agamemnon had been killed, also following choral anapests (*Ag.* 1331–42), he had spoken sentences (*Ag.* 1343, 45). Aegisthus instead echoes the cries of the raving Cassandra (*Ag.* 1072, 76 *ototototoi*, 1114 *e e*), inarticulate and possibly effeminate shouts[7] that cause the chorus to stand back, away from the door and within the *orchēstra* (872–74). The chorus of

Libation Bearers helps shape the narrative: they interfered with Cilissa and here they anticipate the coming action. This is much more control than the chorus exerted in *Agamemnon*, and begins to anticipate the chorus' increased prominence in *Eumenides*. The disparaging presentation of Aegisthus in the first play is here magnified by the haste with which he is dispatched. The audience does not mourn his death: this is merely one step towards the killing of Clytaemestra.

New characters continue to appear: now a Servant cries out ready to serve the function of a messenger and to relate that his master has been killed. Panicked, the household slave calls for help, especially protection from a young man (879; this probably indicates that the servant is visibly older); yet his speech remains unfocused as he berates himself (881–2). He is looking specifically for Clytaemestra (882), which is why he asks for the bolts to the women's quarters to be opened (878). Despite the offbeat tone of the scene, this request causes considerable problems for understanding the stage action of the play, since it has been taken to mean that there is a second (visible) doorway onstage, from which Clytaemestra appears, the action of the play having imperceptibly shifted to an interior space within the palace of Argos.[8] As discussed (Chapter 1.3), there are no other places in Greek tragedy that demand more than one door, and so this interpretation requires unparalleled stage resources. By the time the Servant appears, the central door has been used six times.[9] When doors have been mentioned (*LB* 561, 571, 653) the reference is to the central *skēnē* door. Aeschylus imagines a detailed and realistic interior space, in which men and women have separate domestic areas (as at 712, which refers to the men's quarters), and this helps spectators imagine the events taking place just out of their sight.[10] When the Servant calls for the door to the women's quarters to be opened (878), perhaps the audience is asked to imagine that the setting has shifted to the interior of the household court (in which case, if there is a second door, it would be from there that Clytaemestra emerges at 885), or it must accept the inconsistency that the Servant exits the palace and the instructions are meant to be heard through the walls.

Neither of these explanations is needed, and a third possibility presents itself: the servant begins by shouting within the house (875–80), and emerges to continue the speech outside (881–4). Within the house, his confused cries and banging maintain the reality of the imagined interior space, evoking both the domestic staff and interior walls. Once he emerges from the palace, the question of Clytaemestra's location is addressed technically to the chorus in the *orchēstra* but delivered out to the audience: "'Where is Clytaemestra? What is she doing?' (882). Justice (884 *Dikēs*) is acting, and behind the servant, appearing again in the main doorway of the house, stands Clytaemestra.

This is not the only way in which the scene can be staged, but to my mind this proposal removes the performance objections that have been raised, and means that *Libation Bearers* is performable in the same minimalist space as seems to be expected elsewhere in the fifth century. There is no need to imagine an unparalleled (and unsignalled) shift to an interior space.

4.4 Pylades

The Servant emerges from the doorway (881); Clytaemestra follows him (885); the servant returns to the palace when Clytaemestra gives him an instruction (889); Orestes appears (891), and is followed by Pylades. This is the busiest sequence of action in any extant tragedy, and Aeschylus uses it to orchestrate another *coup de théâtre*. The pace of the play has been increasing: while no new characters were introduced between lines 10 and 656, and in less than half that time the audience has met the Doorkeeper (657), Clytaemestra (668), Cilissa (730), Aegisthus (838), and the Servant (875). The effect is kaleidoscopic, and these staccato scenes build to the present moment.

Clytaemestra has awoken and emerged from the women's quarters, and followed the Servant outside. It is night-time: night was approaching when Orestes entered the palace (660–2, 710–11) and everyone was asleep (881–2).[11] Is her costume different than it was earlier, or the hair on the mask tied up for bed?[12] Possibly, but this is not needed. The effect is almost dream-like: the slave speaks in riddles (886: 'I say the dead one is killing the living'),[13] but Clytaemestra interprets it instantly, and calls for an axe. It is a no-nonsense response: she is going to deal with this. The Servant, who unlike the chorus is aligned with the queen, runs in to obey. Two lines later, Orestes appears, holding a bloodstained sword. Normally in tragedy, such entrances are announced,[14] but Clytaemestra's control of the threshold is disrupted, and Orestes stands in the position of power that she has previously controlled. He threatens her and, in a moment of unguarded realism, her first thought is not for herself, but for Aegisthus (893).[15] She is vulnerable, and calls for her husband. Orestes' cruel response is instinctive and diverts him from his mission: 'You love the man? In that case, you will lie in the same grave …' (894–5).

The exchange that follows is crucial for understanding the play and the tetralogy (*LB* 896–903):

Clyt.:   Hold, my son, and, child, respect this
         breast, from which often, indeed, while dozing,
         you suckled nourishing milk with your gums.

Orestes: Pylades, what shall I do? Should I be ashamed to kill my
           mother?

Pylades: What then would remain of the oracles of Loxias   900
           declared by the Pythian [*puthochrēstos*], and trusted,
           well-made oaths?
           Make all men your enemies, rather than the gods.

Orestes: I judge you the victor, and you advise me well . . .

Orestes finally uses the word 'mother' (899 *mēter*'), a word he has avoided until now; only when presented with the reality of his own mother's breast, he hesitates. The brief passage raises many questions, and means that the precise meaning is unclear and different spectators might legitimately reach different conclusions about what is transpiring.

Clytaemestra bares her breast, offering it to Orestes in a gesture that is designed to provoke his pity. It is a powerful gesture, one that resonates directly with Hecuba's appeal from the walls of Troy in *Iliad* 22.79–89. There, she is about to lose her son, and the maternal appeal recalls poignantly the mother-child bond. In Aeschylus, the gesture is much more ambiguous. The audience is uncertain whether Clytaemestra is sincerely pleading or attempting once more to manipulate men to survive. A strong case can be made either way: human motivations are obscure, and it is possible that she might not even distinguish between these two. The decision made about *LB* 691–9 is relevant (see Chapter 3.5): if Clytaemestra delivered that speech, the audience has already seen the queen unguarded, and can use that as a baseline against which to evaluate the present response. If that was Electra, Clytaemestra's automatic loving and protective reaction at the news of Aegisthus' death (893) has only a few lines earlier served a similar function, if on a smaller scale.[16]

Great theatre revels in this sort of ambiguity. The first half of the play was motivated through Clytaemestra's nightmare of the previous evening, which presented a serpent drawing blood from her nursing breast. Now Orestes stands before her. The dream image and the intimate detail of the child dozing at the breast here suggest that Clytaemestra at one time was nurturing and loving to her son, and that she perceives herself as a nursing mother.[17] That seems psychologically plausible, even if it appears to make modern assumptions about how Aeschylus is drawing his characters. Problematically, the image of the dozing child equally recalls the intimate details in

Cilissa's caring description. In reality, there is no need to choose: both realities can be 'true' within the fictional world, in that both women may have nursed the infant Orestes. For the audience, though, one possibility will seem more plausible in the moment, and it is not sure which it will be. Cilissa had emphasized the queen's duplicity (737–41), and she claims to have 'nourished' Orestes (750 *ethrepsa*), having received him from his mother.[18] Clytemnestra is desperately fighting for her life and makes a consciously artificial appeal that is challenged by the nurse's direct claim.

Aeschylus keeps the nurse in the story (also present in Stesichorus and Pindar), but her presence in the light of this scene is not a straightforward hold-over from the tradition: Cilissa's presence challenges the underlying assumptions in Clytaemestra's maternal appeal. As Whallon writes, 'There is in any case no reason to give credence to Clytemnestra's words, since she is an adept at grand deception'.[19] Further, the practical implications call for a male actor to appeal to a female breast. Does the actor wear padding, an under-costume as in comedy? There is no other evidence for such bodysuits in tragedy, and it is unlikely to make a difference given the scale of the theatre. We must avoid any impulse to downplay the gesture or to import modern senses of modesty to disrupt Aeschylus' *coup de théâtre*.[20] Regardless, the audience is drawn to juxtapose male/female, and this in its way resonates with the initial characterization of Clytaemestra as androgynous (*Ag.* 11). The possibility that the scene calls attention to the moment's overt theatricality, as will again happen momentarily with Pylades, cannot be discounted.

What, then, does Orestes' hesitation mean? His decision has been fixed since he has appeared on stage, and through Electra, the *kommos*, and the staging of the necromancy, the play has presented the young hero pursuing justice for Agamemnon undeterred. Until now. The true horror of what he is about to do hits him, and he pauses, sword in hand. Whatever Clytaemestra's intention, the appeal is momentarily effective. Faced with the need to re-affirm his decision, Orestes turns to his companion Pylades and asks for advice. This move is startling, if only because of Pylades' silence throughout the play. Aeschylus regularly had characters onstage but silent: a visual presence onto which the audience must imagine the inner workings of thought since nothing is given voice. Aristophanes' *Frogs* 911–21 isolates Achilles in *Myrmidons* and the title character in *Niobe* as prominent examples of this theatrical device, though Cassandra in *Agamemnon* is another. Pylades is different:

> this silence is not significant; no attention has been paid to it. . . . The lines gain extra weight and impact precisely because Pylades has never spoken before. It is not the silence that matters, but the ending of it.[21]

There's more to it here, because the audience thinks that Pylades cannot speak, within the frame of the Rule of Three Actors. Orestes, Clytaemestra, and the Servant have all spoken within the previous 20 lines, and possibly (depending on the assignment of *LB* 691–9) there has been a three-speaker scene earlier in the play in which Pylades was on stage. The audience has been led to believe that the third speaking actor is used for another role, and then suddenly Pylades is asked a question that demands an answer. For the actor it requires a quick change of costume and mask (the Servant leaves at 889; Orestes appears at 892, and we would expect Pylades to be with him, possibly after 893 when Orestes points back to the house). Since Pylades has been Orestes' constant companion, there is not a lot of wiggle room, and it appears the actor is being asked to perform a lightning costume change.[22] Aeschylus creates misdirection, and for those spectators following the role division, it is possible they will be duped. The rapidity of movement, in and out of the same door, invites the audience to make assumptions: it's a kind of theatrical shell game, and the quicker the costume change, the more impressive the effect.

Pylades' answer is a good one: the oracles of Apollo take precedence, and one should respect the gods before human beings. In fact, it's a great answer: in *Agamemnon* the king had faced a decision immediately before his death. That play presented a teasing *stichomythia* between him and Clytaemestra (*Ag.* 931–6), in which she gets him to admit that walking on the tapestries, defiling the wealth of his house, is something he might have vowed to do and that Priam, the king of Troy, hypothetically would have performed in victory.[23] That he didn't make such a vow is suppressed, but Clytaemestra plays to his vanity, saying, 'Do not feel ashamed [*aidestheis*] before the censure of mortals' (*Ag.* 937). The verb is the same one Orestes uses (*LB* 900 *aidesthō*), and there is a theologically correct answer for Agamemnon: *what would then become of divine oracles and oaths? I should make all men my enemies rather than the gods.* Had Agamemnon said that, heeding the gods and not walking on tapestries, he might have lived. Instead he thinks not of the gods, but the mob: 'Truly, report coming from the people has great strength' (*Ag.* 938); and with that he is doomed. Seven years later, Orestes has Pylades to guide him, and Orestes is reminded of the importance of the gods – and Apollo hasn't lied before (*LB* 559). Pylades speaks the answer that Agamemnon had failed to give, and the fittingness of the sentiment apparently affirms Orestes sufficiently to kill his mother. The surprise use of the third actor coincides with the turning-point of the narrative, and with the return of the voice of Apollo (echoing the surprise use of the third actor in *Agamemnon* with Cassandra). With all of the athletic metaphors that have been employed, drawn from different sports, and the repeated urging for 'victory' at choral speech-ends (478 *nikēi*, 868 *nikēi*), it is fitting that Orestes grants Pylades victory here (903 *nikan*).[24]

This moment of hesitation is the second scene in the play that entered the artistic tradition. Two vases survive that show Clytaemestra holding forth her breast to Orestes.[25] On the earlier one, an Athenian red-figure kalpis in Nafplion dating to *c.* 440, Clytaemestra sits on an altar before a heroic Orestes, while a young woman flees in panic. As with the scene at the tomb (Chapter 2.2), this is not an illustration of the stage event, but it does draw on and reconfigure elements that seem to emerge directly from the theatrical tradition. I would not, for example, suggest that Clytaemestra is actually sitting on the *thymelē* or a stage altar at this point; rather the presence of the altar is a visual symbol of her attitude of supplication. The other woman is perhaps meant to be understood as Electra, even though she is not on stage at this point of the play. This vase thereby focuses on a mother's appeal, and the different responses from her children. Whoever the woman is, her flight signals the threat that Orestes poses. Unfortunately, damage to the body of Orestes and the head of Clytaemestra mean that the vase is less visually compelling than it will originally have been. The later vase, a Paestan neck-amphora from the 330s at the Getty Museum (*RVP* 2/418), has been reproduced on the cover of this book. The struggle between Orestes and his mother suggests a physical altercation, and in the upper right of the image the presence of an Erinys threatens the eventual fate of Orestes.

Following Pylades' advice, Orestes and Clytaemestra fall into the regular rhythms of *stichomythia*, with Clytaemestra pleading, and Orestes confidently countering every verbal thrust from his mother. She eventually accedes to the inevitable (922–30, in a very literal rendering):

Clyt.:   You seem, my child, about to kill your mother.

Orestes: Not I, but you are killing yourself.

Clyt.:   Look! Guard against your mother's malignant hounds.

Orestes: Failing this, how shall I flee those of my father?   925

Clyt.:   While alive, I seem to sing my dirge in vain, to a tomb.

Orestes: Yes, my father's blood sets this fate for you.

Clyt.:   Ah me! This was the snake I bore and nourished [*ethrepsamēn*].
         The fear from dreams was a true prophet.

Orestes: You slew him you should not, so suffer what you
         should not.   930

The final four lines from the *koryphaios* (931–4) accompany Orestes and Pylades leading Clytaemestra into the house. Clytaemestra calls herself mother twice; Orestes invokes his father twice. The hounds in 924 are the Erinyes of Clytaemestra, answered in 925 by those of Agamemnon. Clytaemestra interprets her dream, and her final couplet, ruminating on its meaning and interrupting the rhythm of *stichomythia*, will prove to be her final words.[26]

4.5 Bloodguilt

The stakes of Orestes' choice have been fully described, and the choral song that follows will push the audience to meditate on the implications for bloodguilt. Within the Aeschylean perspective of these plays, the Erinyes are hounds that hunt those who slay their kin, acquiring bloodguilt. It is not a subjective thing: they are forces of the universe, chthonic powers, whose office is clear and inescapable. Even if this is a completely new understanding of their powers, originating in this play (as indeed seems likely), the playwright has laid out the parameters and the theological implications of bloodguilt and revenge as they operate in the dramatic world.

It is not the case that Orestes doesn't have a choice. He does; it just happens to be between two very unpleasant alternatives. The alternatives are virtually indistinguishable in their outcomes: either way, he becomes the quarry for Erinyes – those of his father or those of his mother. Though we have free will, Zeus does not always allow everyone a portion of happiness (*Iliad* 24.527–33). Within the moral universe of the play, matricide is not a clearly better choice. When Orestes asks, 'What should I do?' (899), it is a recognition that there is no correct answer. Even if he obeys Apollo, honours his father, and becomes his avenger as is his obligation as the closest male kin, he will nonetheless be guilty of matricide. This inevitability is the basis of revenge, Justice (*Dikē*), in *Libation Bearers*, and spectators must appreciate the ineluctable nature of Orestes' situation if they are to understand the legalistic slippages that occur in *Eumenides*. The trial he faces there provides an artificial release from an inescapable dilemma.

The contrast with the situation in *Agamemnon* is pronounced. Agamemnon returns from Troy and is lured to his death, deceived and flattered by his wife. The choice to walk upon the tapestries is foolish, and is symbolic of his willingness to kill Iphigenia (a psychologically plausible reason for Clytaemestra to want to kill him) and his own sacrilege at Troy (as the gods use his wife as a punishing agent or *alastōr*). His family curse continues to work itself out across generations (a theme raised implicitly every time he is called a son of Atreus or a Pleisthenid). Though we can say he might have known better, Agamemnon is shown to be a fool killed by an unfaithful wife and her lover. Orestes in contrast returns from exile urged by Apollo to kill his mother. The choice he makes is between two undesirable realities. It too is a working out of the family curse.

The final choral song of the play (*LB* 935–71) recognizes this tension of bloodguilt. Again, the poet uses the unusual device of mesodes to interrupt clear strophic responsion. Two triads (A, mes α, A', B, mes β, B') preserve the pattern from the last stasimon, even if its irregularity prevents the audience from feeling comfortable with the musical shape of the play. Justice (935 *dika*) came to Troy, and now it comes to Argos. Orestes and Pylades are presumably the double lion,[27] the double Ares (938; cf. 461 *Arēs Arei xumbalei, Dikai Dika*, 'Ares clashes with Ares, Justice with Justice'), but Orestes is also 'the quarry declared by the Pythian god' (940 *ho puthochrēstos fugas*), as the chorus repeats an unusual word used by Pylades (*LB* 901). I prefer to see *phugas* as an inversion of the powerful image of the lion: the word identifies Orestes as both an exile who has now returned and as something that hounds would hunt. The first mesode declares victory over the two offenders-deserving-vengeance (944), i.e. Clytaemestra and Aegisthus.[28] The *antistrophē* exalts 'cunning-minded Punishment' (947 *doliophrōn Poina*), a line that in the corresponding *strophē* had characterized the penalty paid at Troy as 'a punishment with heavy justice' (936 *barudikos poina*). The precise echo of the repeated *poina* in the last two syllables of the line is deliberate, and the shift from abstract noun to personification subtle. Aeschylus preserves the impact of the word *barudikos*, since the remainder of the *antistrophē* provides an etymological pun for *Dikē*, with the *Di-* in *Dikē* supposedly coming from from *Dios kora* (949 'Zeus's daughter'). This is a false etymology, but it affirms that justice is not simply a concern for Zeus, but it is his daughter and his namesake.[29]

The second triad in the song returns the audience to Clytaemestra and the present situation. In the *strophē*, Loxias (953) at Delphi, another Olympian god allied with Orestes, declares without cunning that the queen will be killed with cunning (955 *adolōs dolia*). The Greek word order is flexible enough for the two words to be juxtaposed against one another in an apparent paradox. The mesode suggests a racehorse has been allowed to run free, as the house will rise up and be restored. Central to that process will be Orestes appearing from the front door of the house (966), having ritually purified its interior. This is a striking way to describe Orestes murdering his mother, but it is the perspective of the chorus, which now, as in previous songs, is representing not only its perspective as slaves who have offered libations to Agamemnon, but on behalf of the city of Argos as a whole. In that sense, chorus members are recapitulating the authority with which they spoke in *Agamemnon*.

At this point, the audience is expecting a scream: would that the house could take voice (*Ag.* 34–5). There is no doubt that Clytaemestra is being killed. Agamemnon screamed; Aegisthus screamed. Aeschylus has created the necessary circumstances for a third scream here, but it never comes. The silence of Clytaemestra is apparently the final element in her characterization: she does not call for help or yell in pain, but accepts the inevitable with a kind of dignity.

4.6 Humour and Tragedy

Libation Bearers offers a sustained engagement with human suffering and human inability in a world of arbitrary and capricious gods. In particular, it isolates the mental suffering of what appears to be a hopeless choice, one that is cosmically unfair. As a tragedy, the plot presents an extreme situation that nonetheless explores a universal human question about how to behave when ethical injunctions are in conflict with each other. Orestes makes a choice, but it is not obviously the right one, and it cannot be justified in the light of the events of *Eumenides*. At this point in the *Oresteia*, his decision is terrible. Orestes has not wavered until the last moment, but in doing so he shows himself to be an ordinary young man, facing a reality that is painfully real. Even if the result is divinely preordained and narratively inevitable, the plot Aeschylus presents becomes almost a roadmap for Athenian tragedy.

The tone of the play is not relentlessly bleak, however. Indeed, there are a number of moments, particularly between the *kommos* and the murders, in which Aeschylus appears to interrupt the unfolding of his tragedy with elements of lightness, features that if not necessarily funny in themselves are decidedly unusual, and would become typical of comedy by the end of the century. This is not to say that they generated laughter (they didn't), but their inclusion shifts the overall tone of the middle of the play. This has not been generally recognized, in part because any individual instance can be downplayed, and in part because of the lack of comparison material for the early part of the century. Nevertheless, the combined weight, when measured against expected tragic norms (as known from the surviving works of Aeschylus alone, or including those of Sophocles and Euripides) becomes substantial.

A quick review of the play so far will identify a dozen such features, in which the potential for humour may be thought to exist:

1. Eavesdropping. Orestes and Pylades eavesdrop on Electra and the chorus during the *parodos*. Eavesdropping is not in itself comedic, but it does point to the artificiality of theatre: it is a means for one or more characters to gain knowledge revealed unintentionally by another, and so it creates a power differential that can subsequently be exploited. The spectators remain in the know, and possess the same superior information as the eavesdropper(s). This encourages identification with those characters. While eavesdropping is found in subsequent tragedy (e.g. Euripides' *Hippolytus*), it is primarily associated with the New Comedy of Greece and Rome.

2. Recognition. While Aeschylus could not have anticipated the response his scene would receive in subsequent tragedy, the direct engagement with the three Aeschylean tokens in Euripidean drama, and in *Electra* 518–44 in particular, demonstrates that the scene possessed the potential for humour.

3. *Kommos*. We cannot know how the elaborate architecture of the *kommos* was expressed musically and choreographically, but it is clear that in *Libation Bearers* Aeschylus introduces complex patterns that serve to frustrate audience expectations of what

is to come. The use of mesodes and syncopated structural rhythms (here and in subsequent stasima), with the irregular alteration of voices in lyric passages, is both disorienting and exhilarating for spectators.

4. Anticlimax. Following the long and insistent invocation of Agamemnon's ghost, the possibility that some spectators will be momentarily disoriented when it fails to appear is real.

5. Etymological puns. Puns are made on the names of Pylades (561–2 *pyla* | *Pyladēi*), Clytaemestra (651 *kluta*), and Justice (949 *Dios kora Dikan*). Again, this is a feature found later in tragedy,[30] but the repetition calls attention to subsequent examples, and consequently the etymology of Justice feels the most forced.

6. Door-knocking. The introduction of the ordinary elements of everyday life in a way that diminishes the elevated status of the figures of tragedy is potentially funny. Door-knocking scenes are common in comedy, and the closest parallel in tragedy comes from Euripides' *Helen* 436–7, which is anti-heroic and self-consciously bathetic. The single line spoken by the Doorkeeper, whether or not the character remains unseen, further marks the scene as unusual.

7. Cilissa. The unexpected appearance of Orestes' wet nurse is both endearing and intimate, again challenging the elevated tone of tragedy. Her apparently honest self-presentation contradicts the information that has come from Clytaemestra, and reinforces audience sympathies with Orestes. For Murray, she is 'ludicrous in her tears'.[31] As part of her portrayal, she introduces urination and dirty diapers, bringing banal, everyday realities into the account of the meaning of justice for all humanity.

8. Interference. The *koryphaios* then changes the direction of the plot, altering the message that Aegisthus receives. The unnamed

libation bearer, an Asiatic slave in service to the house, is the reason that Orestes is able to achieve his revenge.

9. Aegisthus. The short scene with Aegisthus, as he returns supremely confident and gloating at the news he has been told, totally unaware of the danger that threatens him, means that his self-perception (as regent and individual most in control) is in greatest conflict with his reality (as sacrificial victim bringing himself to slaughter). The sudden diminishment of those with inflated self-esteem is another feature of extant comedy, and not naturally part of the tragic register.

10. Servant. Between the Doorkeeper, Aegisthus, the Servant, and Pylades, *Libation Bearers* offers four of the briefest speaking roles in tragedy. Having characters enter and exit repeatedly, during an episode (and not only at the beginning and end of choral songs), is again a feature typical of later comedy, and is much rarer in tragedy. Role doubling is an established practice in the Athenian theatre, but the rapid shifting between many characters finds its closest parallel in Aristophanes' *Birds* (414). The Phrygian slave in Euripides' *Orestes* (408) is a much developed version of this character, and is played for comedy.

11. Costume change. This momentum reaches a climax as the Servant actor changes within a few lines back into Pylades. At this point, Aeschylus is actively trying to trick his audience.[32]

12. Doors. All of the confusion about the interior space and the number of doors visible on stage indicates the instability that Aeschylus is creating in the dramatic world.[33]

All of these examples are funny, in one sense of the word or another. While Aeschylus was not playing them for laughs, each moment in this list represents something potentially transgressive to the genre of tragedy. This goes beyond straightforward generic experimentation: even if some instances are removed from consideration, many indications remain that as Aeschylus draws Orestes inevitably closer to his horrific act, he is destabilizing the world around him.

Modern scholars are more comfortable assigning generic confusion of this sort to the later playwright Euripides than to Aeschylus. The tone of Euripides' plays shifts in the 410s significantly, and this leads to the articulation of certain qualities to be associated with the separate playwrights in the literary debate between a fictionalized Aeschylus and Euripides in Aristophanes' *Frogs*. The character Euripides boasts that characters of both sexes and all classes could speak, whether woman, slave, master, maiden, or old woman (*Frogs* 949–50); this was 'democratic' (952). Further, he introduced 'domestic matters' (959 *oikeia pragmata*) to tragedy.[34] Cilissa introduces *oikeia pragmata* too, and ironically the appeal of this play in the later fifth century may have been in part due to its anticipation of what came to be seen as a Euripidean quality.[35]

Repeated theatrical surprises and a lightness of tone amidst the gruesomeness of matricide, and particularly the vascillation between humour and tragedy, are difficult to achieve and to describe. There are, of course, parallels, the most obvious of which in English theatre is the Porter scene in *Macbeth* (Act 2, Scene 3). Shakespeare's drunken Porter slowly responds to the incessant knocking at the castle door. The scene immediately follows the murder of Duncan by Macbeth and Lady Macbeth. Among other things, the Porter scene contains door-knocking, a servant being introduced unexpectedly at the darkest moment of the play and frank discussion of bodily fluids ('And drink, sir, is a great provider of three things … nose-painting, sleep, and urine'). In his description of the Porter scene, Thomas De Quincey noted his youthful sense that 'the knocking at the gate, which succeeds the murder of Duncan, produced for my feelings an effect for which I could never account: the effect was—that it reflected back upon the murder a peculiar awfulness and a depth of solemnity'.[36] The Porter scene casts the darkness of regicide and the killing of a guest into relief through the introduction of contrast, thereby offering comic relief.

De Quincey is clear that the purpose is neither escape nor denial: a poet 'must throw the interest on the murderer: our sympathy must be with *him*'.[37] Since 'the murderers are taken out of the region of human things, human purposes, human desires … cut off by an immeasurable gulph from the ordinary tide and succession of human affairs', the knocking at the gate and the comedy of the scene mean 'the human has made its reflux upon the fiendish'.[38] This is the effect of all the unusual features in *Libation Bearers* – a peculiar awfulness. In Aeschylus, they precede the climactic killing (there is much evil yet to be done in Shakespeare's Scotland), but the effect of the contrast created is the same. Aeschylus must strike a balance in his presentation of Orestes: 'The killing of Clytemnestra must remain viscerally appalling, while it is yet in this particular instance not ethically repellent, and Aeschylus achieves this contradictory effect with an appeal to the rules of reciprocity that governed parents and children'.[39] The matricide in *Libation Bearers* threatens to destabilize the entire tragic world view. Aeschylus has set himself an ethical problem from which the play will not offer a means of escape.

4.7 Furies

Gilbert Murray wrote of the last hundred lines of *Libation Bearers*, 'This marvelous scene scarcely needs comment'.[40] Some scholars are hilarious. In this final section, a number of visual symbols are presented, each of which represents Aeschylus' closing contribution to larger themes he has developed so far in the *Oresteia*. At the end of the choral song, the doors to the palace of Argos open and the *ekkyklēma* rolls into view. 'Behold the twin tyrants of this land',

Orestes declares (973). On the *ekkyklēma* stands Orestes over the
corpses of Aegisthus and Clytaemestra.[41] The horrors perpetuated
in the darkness of the house are thrust into the light for all to see. A
killer, sword in hand, standing over male and female bodies is what
the audience saw at *Agamemnon* 1372. Aeschylus thereby introduces another mirror scene,[42] as the poet creates a visual echo in
order to allow the audience to interpret the *tableau* it sees. The son
of Clytaemestra stands where she had, fulfilling her prophetic dream
and assuming the place she has left vacant at the door of the *skēnē*. At
the same time, however much Orestes has sought to distance himself
from his mother, their shared blocking undermines any moral
victory that the audience might wish to ascribe to the avenger. He,
like his mother before him, is a murderer.

'Behold again', he says, repeating the same verb (973 *idesthe*, 980
idesthe), the device (981 *mēchanēma*) that had bound the hands
and feet of Agamemnon. There are no shortage of stage properties
brought onstage in this final scene (this too is a technique found
in later comedy). The device is a blood-purple robe that is spread
out from the mouth of the doorway, pouring into the *orchēstra*. In
Agamemnon, the returning king had walked on tapestries, destroying
the wealth of his own house. Whatever fabric was used for that scene
had also served as the enveloping net that had wrapped Agamemnon
in the bathtub where he was killed.[43] The same fabric is brought back
as the symbol of Agamemnon's death and of the final victory over his
killers. Orestes gives instructions to attendants to spread the fabric
out, revealing it to Zeus. Possibly, Orestes' garments are also spattered
with blood, but given the scale of the theatre, a lot of blood would be
needed to ensure anything was visible.[44] Aeschylus produces symbols
for his audience, not in defiance of logic, but with a forced logic:
he wants the tapestries to be seen again, redeployed as a new visual
representation of his imagery.

There will be a third imperative: 'And now see me ...' (1034 *kai nun horate me ...*). Orestes indicates the olive branch that he holds in his hand, which has remained visible and unexplained since his emergence. The olive branch is a puzzle for spectators to interpret, one that is eventually explained as a marker of his future existence as a suppliant of Apollo (1034–6). This anticipates the opening scene of *Eumenides*, which is set at Delphi, Apollo's shrine. Earlier, Orestes had imagined Zeus could serve as a witness (987 *martus*) for him, correctly anticipating his forthcoming trial, while placing ultimate responsibility for events on father Zeus.[45]

The sequence of Orestes' speech is confused, but the themes are clear and reinforced by stage properties: the corpses (973–9), the robe, with Zeus as witness (980–90, 997–1004), Clytaemestra (991–6, 1005–6). This in fact is the order that is accepted by both West and Sommerstein for this speech, moving the continued description of the robe (997–1004) before lines 991–6.[46] Orestes describes his mother as a moray eel or snake (994 *echidn'*), which admittedly might be seen as an excessive underlining of the point of her dream at this point in the play.

The variability of tone which has characterized the entire revenge action continues, and suddenly the chorus begins chanting anapests, accompanied by screams lamenting the fallen tyrants and predicting future suffering for Orestes (1007–9, 1018–20): the cycle of revenge begins anew, unexpectedly.[47] This upsets Orestes, and he emphasizes the aptness of his revenge: Aegisthus' sword (presumably that used by Clytaemestra in *Agamemnon*) dyed the garment spread before him with blood. It too becomes a sign of the ongoing suffering for his family, the 'pollution from this victory' (1017 *nikēs tēsd' ... miasmata*). Orestes' next speech positions him as an out-of-control charioteer (1022–3, no longer the orphaned colt of 794–9), and he feels he is losing his senses (1024 *phrenes*) as personified Fear (1024 *Phobos*) and Frenzy (1025 *Kotōi*) become mobilized (1026–8):

While I am still in my senses [*emphrōn*], I announce to my friends [*philois*]
And say that not without Justice [*ouk aneu dikēs*] I killed my mother,
The polluted [*miasma*] father-killer, detested by the gods.

Orestes declares that Apollo, Loxias, led him to do this, and that
he added a further inducement: if Orestes killed his mother, he
would remain 'without blame for the evil deed' (1031 *ektos aitias
kakēs*). This is news. When Orestes first mentioned his consultation
of Apollo (see Chapter 2.3, *LB* 269–6), and when he was facing his
mother and on the point of hesitation (see Chapter 4.4, *LB* 900–2,
or 924), the audience (and Electra, and the chorus) did not know
that he would have Apollo's protection. That information is delayed
until 1031.[48] This is a dramaturgical convenience, since the stakes
of the conflict would be reduced if the audience knew this information. Normally, it might invite an attentive spectator to re-assess
the dramatic action. Orestes declares his victory. He is rational and
clear-headed as he describes his decision to go, with an olive-branch
wrapped in wool, to Delphi: ritual purity awaits him in the action
of *Eumenides* (1034–9). He even has the sense to signal the eventual
arrival of Menelaus in Argos (1040–3), which also looks forward in
the tetralogy, anticipating the action of the satyr-play *Proteus*, which
tells the story of Menelaus' *nostos*.[49]

This could be a satisfying ending to the play: the speech of the
koryphaios (1044–7) declares Argos liberated, and concludes praising
Orestes for 'luckily cutting the heads of the two serpents' (1047 *duoin
drakontoin eupetōs temōn kara*). The word *eupetōs* is a metaphor from
playing dice, and matricide is seemingly relegated to a lucky throw.[50]
Until the world breaks.

Orestes suddenly sees the Erinyes of his mother, who have come
to claim their due: a multitude (1057) of women that look like
Gorgons (1048), wearing dark tunics (1049), wreathed in snakes
(1050 *drakousin*), eyes dripping with pus (1058). It a horrific, frightening description. Technically, Orestes is not going mad. To the

eyes of the chorus his behaviour seems insane: to them these are 'fantasies' (1051, 1053 *doxai*). The audience knows better. Within the theological world constructed, these supernatural beings are real and are now activated against Orestes. They are 'my mother's malignant hounds' (1054 *mētros enkotoi kunes*, exactly the phrase used by Clytaemestra at 924), the Erinyes. By calling them Gorgons, Orestes recapitulates the image of Perseus at *LB* 831–7, and their frightful features recall the earlier descriptions of them as blood-drinkers (*Ag.* 1186–93, *LB* 577–8). Orestes calls on Apollo (1057), but Apollo lied to Orestes, and the onset of this vision serves as Orestes' realization of the truth (remember *LB* 559, 'Lord Apollo, a prophet who has not lied previously'). Aeschylus takes away the comfortable conclusion at 1047. Victory turns instantly to defeat, and the vision of his mother's furies drives Orestes out of the performance area. His last words are emphatic (1061–2):

> You do not see them. I see them.
> I am driven away, no longer can I stay.

The emphasis on vision evokes the insistent imperatives of sight he has used throughout this scene (973, 980, 1029, 1034). The *koryphaios* tries to reassure him, but Orestes continues uncontrolled, presumably scrambling wildly through the *orchēstra* as he flees the Erinyes. Orestes runs offstage, being pursued by his tormentors, to become an exile once again.

What does the audience see in the final moments of this play? Most scholars assume that the audience sees what the chorus sees: an apparently maddened Orestes, no longer in his senses (1026 *emphrōn*) fleeing an unseen foe. If this is so, it is yet another circumstance unique to the play, for nowhere else (except the gadfly that pursues Io in *Prometheus Bound*) do beings exist in the dramatic world that are unseen by members of the audience. Normally, audience perspective is accurate: Athena in *Ajax* and the frogs in *Frogs* are embodied presences on stage, seen by the spectators but not by the characters.[51] Further, the identity of the chorus in *Eumenides* is going to be as embodied Erinyes, who will be domesticated into the Athenian ritual system as Eumenides, the Kindly Ones. Given this, it is worth at least considering whether the Furies appear visibly on stage at the end of *Libation Bearers* – still unseen by the chorus, but pouring from the *skēnē*, and driving Orestes away. This is not a widely held view, but it is productive for thinking about theatrical options available to the playwright and director. Brown presents the clearest case against a bodily appearance by Erinyes:[52] he argues that since *Agamemnon* and *Libation Bearers* have operated entirely without supernatural entities visible, that persists here despite what happens in *Eumenides*. The idea that the Erinyes actually appeared was first suggested in 1835 by K. O. Müller, and since then has been considered probable only by Whallon, for whom line 1061 is decisive:[53] Orestes' insistence that he sees them indicates that the chorus does not, despite their visible presence. There can be no proof, but a few considerations are relevant. First, there is no doubt that the Furies exist in the dramatic world; the question is one regarding stagecraft, not psychology. Second, introducing the Furies at this point represents no additional cost for the *chorēgos*: Erinyes costumes have been made for *Eumenides*, and a dozen unspeaking extras that will become the citizen jury at the Areopagus trial are already waiting backstage for their appearance as a supplemental chorus.[54]

The first appearance of the Furies should be terrifying.[55] Almost certainly, no chorus of this nature had been conceived previously, and Aeschylus may be innovating even in his anthropomorphic presentation, which is unknown previous to 458. The terror caused by the Erinyes' appearance in the *Oresteia* resonated sufficiently that it generated an anecdote suggesting the visceral impact it had on spectators: 'Some say in the presentation of Eumenides [*en tēi epideixei tōn Eumenidōn*] when he brought on the chorus here and there [*sporadēn*], it so frightened the people that the young fainted and women miscarried [*embrua examblōthēnai*]' (*Vita* 9). As with all such theatrical anecdotes, the story does not need to be true to be useful. The frightening appearance is linked to a genuine emotional response from surprise. This is true horror. The question becomes, when is this moment of initial surprise? As conventionally understood, it is as the sleeping bodies rouse themselves 'one at a time' (*sporadēn*) in the *parodos* of *Eumenides*. The audience sees the horrific faces as they shake off the lethargy from Apollo's spell. I suggest that more theatrically effective, and more likely to generate the theatrical anecdote, would be an initial appearance at the end of *Libation Bearers*. Such an entry would be completely unexpected; it would be sudden, and so more likely to cause surprise; and, occupying only the final minute of the play, it would not give the audience enough time to fully process what it was seeing as Orestes flees.

Theatrical anecdotes are important for what they assume. *Vita* 9 assumes that pregnant women and children were in the audience, a fact that must have been true at the time the story developed. It also assumes the proper response to tragedy is a visceral, emotional one. It is reasonable that spectators might be terrified: as Aristotle says in *Poetics* 6, 1449b 26–7, you're supposed to feel pity and fear. The anecdote also tells us something about the first appearance of the Erinyes in the *Oresteia*. Not necessarily in 458: the story could emerge from a later performance and be memorable enough to commemorate with retelling.[56] Nevertheless, 'some say' the chorus appeared *sporadēn* ('here and there', and so not entering in formation but moving throughout the *orchēstra*). The anecdote does refer to a 'chorus', and calls them 'Eumenides', a term that has not been used in the *Oresteia* yet. The meaning therefore does seem to be 'in the presentation of [the play] *Eumenides*'. The possibility that Erinyes appeared at the end of *Libation Bearers* should not be lightly discounted, since it would give the anecdote more point and arguably makes for a more effective conclusion, signalling the supernatural tenor that will drive the third tragedy. Even if this was not the choice that was made in 458, however, it may have been realized in the proposed reperformance in the 420s, or at any point in the long history of the reception of the play thereafter. Considering such possibilities points to the ongoing theatrical power of Aeschylus' play, and the possibility of such a staging remains available to any future director.

The final words of *Libation Bearers* come from the chorus, and acknowledge 'the power of Ruin' (1076 *menos Atēs*). Orestes has fled; the chorus disperses. If Pylades had stood with Orestes on the *ekkyklēma*, he has not been mentioned throughout this scene and the loyal friend has been abandoned at the moment he is needed most. Though Orestes' matricide appeared to signal the return of light and the restoration of the city, in the end darkness has returned to Argos.

Appendix: Ancient Illustrations of *Libation Bearers*

There are many depictions of the events that take place in *Libation Bearers* that survive painted on Athenian and South Italian vases, and in other media, from the fifth and fourth centuries BCE. They cluster around two moments: the recognition between Orestes and Electra, and Clytaemestra's appeal to Orestes. There are roughly thirty vases depicting the meeting (*LIMC* Elektra I, 1–23, 34–41, 47–8, add. 1–8), nine of which are described below; there are considerably fewer of Clytaemestra's appeal that survive. None of these are intended to be a precise illustration of the staging of the play: artists work within their own idiom, with their own conventions, but they are aware of the larger artistic world, including theatrical production. Unlike comedies, stories from tragedies are represented with the same conventions as other heroic or mythological red-figure vase painting, and so male heroes appear naked with idealized bodies, etc., and not dressed as they would appear on stage.

The images are an important component of the reception of the *Oresteia* in antiquity, and these two scenes-types can be distinguished from those representing the death of Aegisthus or showing Clytaemestra with an axe, which begin before 458. For the earliest viewers, these images interpret popular understanding of the myth in the light of the play, focusing on certain details, incorporating ideas from other sources, and adding the artist's individual creative perspective. Illustrations are not snapshots from a production, but a compression of many themes and ideas into a single visual image. They nevertheless constitute an important contemporary understanding of Aeschylus' play.

References and descriptions are very selective but point to further discussions and bibliography.[1]

Abbreviations:

ARV²   Beazley, J. D. 1963. *Attic Red-Figure Vase Painters*, 2nd edn. Oxford.

LCS   Trendall, A. D. 1967. *The Red-Figured Vases of Lucania, Campania, and Sicily*. Oxford.

LIMC *Lexicon Iconigraphicum Mythologicae Classicae.* 8 vols, 1981–2009. Zurich and Munich.

RVAp Trendall, A. D. and A. Cambitoglou. 1978, 1982. *The Red-Figured Vases of Apulia*. 2 vols. Oxford.

RVP   Trendall, A. D. 1987. *The Red-Figured Vases of Paestum*. Oxford.

Recognition

1. Attic Skyphos, 450–430. Attributed to the Penelope Painter. Copenhagen, National Museum of Denmark 597. *ARV²* 1301.5, *LIMC* Elektra I, 34.

    One side of this vase shows Electra and an attendant decorating a three-stepped *stēlē* tomb; the other depicts Orestes and Pylades. The vase was exported from Athens to South Italy and found in Basilicata.

    Prag 1985: 54–6, Taplin 2007: 50n. 8, Hart 2010: 63.

2. Attic Pelike (fragmentary), 380s. Attributed to Jena Painter. University of Exeter, unnumbered. *ARV²* 1516, 80, *LIMC* Elektra I, 1.

    Orestes cuts a lock of his hair at the tomb of Agamemnon

(labelled), with Electra (labelled) holding a *hydria*. Pylades
sits on the tomb holding two spears, and possibly Hermes
and a female attendant (a chorister?) are also visible. The
scene appears to compress both the prologue and the
recognition into a single image. The woman is identified as
Ismene (i.e. Antigone's sister), which Coo suggests is a slip for
Chrysothemis, a sister of Electra and Orestes in the earlier
tradition (2013: 70–2). The vase therefore blends elements
from *Libation Bearers* and Sophocles' *Electra*, and shows
an understanding of the similarities between Electra and
Sophocles' *Antigone*.[2]

Taplin 2007: 50–1, Coo 2013.

3. Apulian Pelike. 410–380. Attributed to the Tarporley Painter or
   his circle.
   Cornell, Johnson Museum 74.74.007.
   LIMC Elektra I, 57.

Electra and Orestes stand on either side of an elaborately
decorated two-step tomb, with an amphora on the top of the
stēlē. Electra holds a tray or basket with a *lekythos* (a vase shape
associated with oil). Orestes on the right leans against a shield,
and pours wine from an *oinochoē*.

Barlow and Coleman 1979.

4. Apulian Krater fragment, 400–375. Black Fury Group.
   Basel, Cahn Coll. HC284.
   RVAp 2/14a, *LIMC* Elektra I, 3.

Electra holds a lock of hair and examines it. There are two
female attendants, one with white hair, and the other holding
an *oinochoē*. Orestes is seated on the tomb, Pylades stands, and
other figures are present but no longer survive.

5. Lucanian Amphora, 380–360. Attributed to the Brooklyn-
    Budapest Painter.
    Naples, Museo Archeologico Nazionale 82140 (H 1755).
    LCS 115/597; *LIMC* Elektra I, 6.

    Orestes and a smaller Pylades approach Electra seated on the
    two-stepped tomb beside an amphora, clearly overcome with
    grief. Behind her an attendant holds a decorated offering box.
    A hero's helm stands on top of the tomb's *stēlē*. Taplin ties the
    moment to Electra's speech at *LB* 84–105. Found in Anzi.

    Taplin 2007: 52–3, Hart 2010: 64.

6. Lucanian Pelike, *c.* 350. Attributed to the Choephori Painter
    (name-vase).
    Paris, Musée du Louvre MNB 167 (K 544).
    LCS 120/599; *LIMC* Elektra I, 7.

    Electra sits at the richly decorated five-step tomb looking out at
    the viewer, with two young men flanking her. One (= Orestes?)
    wears a *pilos* cap and carries a *phialē*. The other (= Pylades?) in
    a *petasos* carries a wreath (as Orestes will at the end of the play)
    and leans against a cadeuceus, associating him with Hermes.

    Taplin 2007: 53–4, Hart 2010: 65.

7. Paestan Neck-Amphora, 350–340. Painter of the Geneva
    Orestes (name-vase).
    Geneva, Musée d'Art et d'Historie HR 29.
    RVP 56/1, *LIMC* Elektra I, 19a.

    Electra, her hair cut short, kneels barefoot at a decorated
    three-step tomb, holding a *phialē*. Two young men, their
    headwear drawn back, approach on either side, balancing the
    composition. Above, also flanking the tomb, are the busts of
    two Erinyes look down. First published in 1984.

Aellen, Cambitoglou, and Chamay 1986: 264–9, Taplin 2007: 54–6.

8. Paestan Neck-Amphora, 340–320. Boston Orestes Painter (name-vase).
   Boston, Museum of Fine Art 99.540.
   RVP 255/1004, *LIMC* Elektra I 19.

   Orestes and Pylades, carrying spears, stand on the ground level at the left of a single-step *stēlē* tomb, while Electra, wearing black and holding an amphora and a dedicatory fillet, stands on the tomb. Her skin is painted white and her hair cropped short. The delicate rendering of her dress is particularly elegant. The presence of two Erinyes in the upper register makes the identification certain.

9. Sicilian Kalyx-Krater, *c*. 380. Dirce Painter.
   Syracuse 36334.
   LCS 203.26, *LIMC* Elektra I, 13.

   Electra sits on an altar with a *stēlē* behind, looking up at Orestes who approaches with a walking stick, his *petasos* drawn back. On the left stands Pylades holding a spear and an attendant with a basket of offerings balanced on her head.

   Prag 1985: 54 (plate 35d).

Clytaemestra's appeal

10. Attic Kalpis, *c*. 440. Attributed to the Polygnotus Group.
    Nauplia 11609/180.
    ARV 1061.154.

    Clytaemestra sits on a plain altar, holding her breast in her left hand and reaching out in supplication with her right to Orestes, who approaches threateningly. On the right, a young woman (Electra? a servant?) flees in terror. This vase deserves to be much better known than it is. It is unfortunately damaged, so that Clytaemestra's face and Orestes' sword hand are no longer extant, but the gesture and narrative context are unmistakable.

Prag 1985: 40–1 (plate 27), Taplin 2007: 275 n. 31.

11. Paestan Neck-Amphora, 340–330. Attributed to the Painter of Würzburg H 5739.
    Malibu, J. Paul Getty Museum 80.AE.155.1.
    RVP 2/418; *LIMC* Klytaimnestra 31.

Clytaemestra kneels before Orestes, cupping her exposed breast in her hand while her right hand knocks away Orestes' sword arm. He appears to be off-balance, and her blow has knocked off his *pilos*, while his left hand seizes her hair. This impression may result from the width of the image being compressed to fit the narrow vase shape. Facial features and hairstyles of mother and son are very similar. To the right, the bust of an Erinys appears with snakes in her hand and hair. A detail of this vase appears on the cover of this book. First published in 1982.

Taplin 2007: 56–7, Hart 2010: 66.

Examples from other media

12–16. Terracotta Relief Plaques, 470–430.
    Paris, Louvre MNB 906, Würzburg H636, Syracuse 24073, Berlin TI 6803, and Louvre S1678.
    LIMC Elektra I, 24–5, 42–3.

These five relief plaques all share the same iconographic

features with the vase-paintings depicting Orestes and Electra at their father's tomb. Louvre MNB 906 and Würzburg H636 show Electra seated at a decorated *stēlē* tomb with an attendant behind her, with Orestes wearing a *pilos* and leading a horse as he approaches the tomb with two attendants. An *oinochoē* is placed prominently by Electra's feet. The fragment from Syracuse shows a similar horse, apparently pressed from the same mould. The remaining examples may show variations of this scene, with apparently Pylades sitting on a step, propping up his chin in his hands, and in one Orestes can be seen leaning against an altar. Arguments about the date of the image are problematically entangled with that of the play. Prag's early dating based on 'un-Aeschylean' elements fails to recognize the freedom artists have to re-interpret scenes: even with a late date, this is not evidence that Orestes and Pylades arrived on horseback. Louvre MNB 906 is said to be from Piraeus (the port of Athens) or the island of Melos; consequently these are referred to as 'Melian' Reliefs. The only certain find-spot is for Syracuse 24073, which was found in Camerina, Sicily.

Jacobsthal 1931, Prag 1985: 51–7, 146–7 (plates 34, 35a–c).

17.   Silver Seal, *c.* 400.
        Ioannina 4279.
        LIMC Klytaimestra 32.

This silver seal shows Clytaemestra on an altar, breast exposed, grappling with Orestes who readies a sword blow. Unlike the vase paintings, she appears here already to have been struck and is wounded in her chest. Both figures are labelled. Found in a tomb in Kérasa, Epirus.

Other scenes

One must be wary of over-interpreting a given illustration, reading a specific version of a mythological narrative into a generic scene: some suggestions made in the past are for scenes too general to make an association with *Libation Bearers* plausible.[3] What distinguishes the scenes above are (a) the continuity of imagery, (b) the presence of details specific to Aeschylus' narrative, including labels, Erinyes, and the offered breast, and (c) the emergence of this imagery in the iconographic tradition after 458. Once established, other relevant details achieve their point, such as the decorated monumental tomb or Orestes' travelling hat. The subsequent repetition and alteration of these details shows the creative innovation of the artists, and a viewer familiar with the play (by reputation, reading, or through performance) may understand more than one not familiar with him.

Many vases depict the death of Aegisthus, an event that takes place in *Libation Bearers* as a preliminary to the conflict between Orestes and Clytaemestra. There is little indication that any of these draw meaningfully on *Libation Bearers*. Instead they reflect the larger tradition that emerges after Stesichorus (see *LIMC* Aigisthos). Even a vase such as Boston 16.1246 (*ARV*[2] 652; *LIMC* Klytaimestra 16), which shows the death of Agamemnon on one side with the death of Aegisthus on the other, is unlikely to reflect Aeschylus.[4] Associated with these are a number of images with Clytaemestra holding an axe: while she calls for one at *LB* 889, the detail is already established in the artistic repertoire by 458 (see *LIMC* Klytaimestra 13–22), and precedes the scene in *Agamemnon*. It may well be a detail that originated in Stesichorus.

Glossary of Greek and Technical Terms

aition	an account providing an origin
anagnōrisis	recognition scene
anapests	chanted verse, often choral, often used for choral entries; an anapestic foot is two short syllables and a long
antistrophē	metrically corresponding stanza ('counterturn') to the preceding *strophē*
astrophic	describing a choral song without strophic responsion (the pairing of *strophē* and *antistrophē*)
aulos	double pipe played by the musician (*aulētēs*) in drama
chous, pl. *choes*	a particular shape of clay vase, a pitcher
dikē	justice, right, penalty
eisodos, pl. *–oi*	one of two side entrances to the *orchēstra*
ekkyklēma	wheeled platform used to reveal interior scenes from inside the *skēnē*
epode	a choral stanza without a metrically corresponding passage, found at the end of a stasimon
Erinys, pl. Erinyes	Fury, supernatural embodiment of avenging blood-guilt
hydria	a particular shape of vase, used for carrying water
kommos	formal lament, sometimes used of lyric dialogue between actor and chorus

koryphaios	chorus leader (lit. 'head-speaker')
libation	a liquid offering to the dead
mesode	a choral stanza without a metrically corresponding passage, placed between a *strophē* and *antistrophē*
nostos	homecoming
oinochoē, pl. *–choai*	a particular shape of clay vase, a wine pitcher
orchēstra	dancing space, part of the performance area of the Greek theatre
parodos	choral entry song
phialē	a shallow bowl for liquid offerings (libations)
philos	friend, ally, family member
scholion, pl. scholia	an interpretative comment from antiquity preserved in the margin of a manuscript
skēnē	stage building, part of the performance area of the Greek theatre
stasimon	choral song
stēlē	an upright column serving as a grave marker
stichomythia	line-by-line storytelling, where dialogue between two characters corresponds to line-ends
strophē	the first of a pair of metrically corresponding stanzas ('turn') in a stasimon
thymelē	altar in the middle of the *orchēstra*
xenos	foreigner, stranger, host/guest

Guide to Further Reading

The edition of Aeschylus in the Loeb Classical Library by Alan Sommerstein (2008a, 2008b) provides the most accessible complete text and translation of the playwright's works, and is accompanied by detailed introductions. A third volume includes the extant fragments (Sommerstein 2008c). For a translation, I encourage students to use Collard 2002, which is clear and accurate, with detailed scholarly notes. There are of course many other translations of the *Oresteia* available, which exhibit different virtues. Richmond Lattimore's 1953 translation has been a mainstay in American university classes, and its most recent edition (Lattimore 2013) includes the fragments of *Proteus*. Solid attempts to supplant it include Fagles 1977, Meineck 1998, Shapiro and Burian 2003 and Sarah Ruden (in Lefkowitz and Romm 2016: 45–177). Individual tastes will consider any of these better or worse for the classroom, or for production. Tony Harrison's aggressive and beautiful poetic version (available in Harrison 2002) was staged at the National Theatre in 1981 and best reflects Aeschylus' startling use of language and imagery. Ted Hughes's spare poetic version (Hughes 1999) is simple and direct, but is not keyed closely to the Greek.

Goldhill 2004 provides an excellent short overview of the tetralogy; Conacher 1987 is also good for readers without Greek, as are guides to the other plays in the tetralogy in this series (Goward 2005 and Mitchell-Boyask 2009). Garvie 1986 is a scholarly commentary on the Greek text of *Libation Bearers*, and it repays any time invested. Bowen 1986 is slighter, but also helpful. The fullest account of the text and its variations is in West 1991. A series of substantial articles have identified and examined a number of crucial themes in the trilogy: Zeitlin 1965 (sacrifice), Fowler 1969: 23–74 (imagery, esp.

of animals and light/dark), Zeitlin 1978 (women), Vidal-Naquet 1981 (hunting), Bowie 1993 (religion and politics), and Griffith 1995 (politics and aristocracy). On *Libation Bearers* itself, see especially Winnington-Ingram 1983: 132–53 ('Orestes and Apollo'), Goldhill 1984: 99–207 ('Definition, paradox, reversal'), Burnett 1998: 99–118 ('Ritualized Revenge'). For the artistic tradition in antiquity, see especially Kossatz-Deissmann 1978, Prag 1985, McPhee 1986, and Morizot 1992 and Dennert 2009. The performance-centred approach adopted here builds on Taplin 1977, 1978, and Wiles 1997.

Selected Chronology

c. 525	Aeschylus' birth at Eleusis (traditional date)
499–496	Aeschylus first competes at Dionysia (traditional date)
490	battle of Marathon
484	Aeschylus' first victory at Dionysia
480	battles of Thermopylae and Salamis
472	Dionysia victory with *Persians*, etc., produced by Pericles
c. 470	Aeschylus travels to Sicily; *Women of Aetna* produced.
468	Sophocles first competes and wins at Dionysia
467	Dionysia victory with *Seven against Thebes*, etc.
467–463	Dionysia victory with *Suppliants*, etc.
458	Dionysia victory with *Oresteia*
c. 456	Aeschylus dies in Sicily.
430s (?)	*Prometheus Bound* produced (at Lenaia?)
420s	Aeschylus' *Oresteia* reperformed in Athens
c. 421	Euripides' *Hecuba*
c. 418 (?)	Euripides' *Electra*
c. 416	Euripides' *Iphigenia among the Taurians*
c. 414 (?)	Sophocles' *Chryses*
c. 412	Sophocles' *Electra*
408	Euripides' *Orestes*
415–405 (?)	reperformance of *Libation Bearers* and *Eumenides* at Lenaia?
406	deaths of Euripides and Sophocles
405	Aristophanes' *Frogs* performed at Lenaia
	Euripides' *Iphigenia in Aulis* performed at Dionysia
386	Performance of 'Old Tragedy' instituted at Dionysia

c. 62 CE	Seneca, *Thyestes*
1155–60	Benoît de Sainte-Maure, *Roman de Troie*
1518	Aldine edition of Aeschylus in Greek
1555	Johannes Sanravius (Jean de Saint-Revy), first Latin trans. of *LB*
1567	Thomas Pikering, *Horestes*
1599	Thomas Dekker and Henry Chettle, *Orestes' Furies* (lost)
1613–18	Thomas Goffe, *The Tragedy of Orestes*
1632	Thomas Heywood, *The Iron Age*, parts I and II
1777	Robert Potter, first English trans. of *LB*
1783	Vittorio Alfieri, *Oreste*
1886	*The Story of Orestes* (dir. George Warr)
1919	Darius Milhaud, *Les Choéphores*
1921	Cambridge Greek Play *The Oresteia*, and film (dir. J. T. Sheppard)
1924	Robinson Jeffers's *The Tower Beyond Tragedy*
1953	Richmond Lattimore's translation published
1958	Martha Graham, *Clytemnestra*
1969	Ferdinando Baldi (dir.), *Il pistolero dell'Ave Maria* (*The Forgotten Pistolero*)
1981	Tony Harrison, *The Oresteia*, National Theatre (dir. Peter Hall)
1990–2	*Les Atrides*, Le Théâtre du Soleil (dir. Ariane Mnouchkine)
1999	Ted Hughes, *The Oresteia*, National Theatre 2000 (dir. Katie Mitchell)
2007	J. K. Rowling, *Harry Potter and the Deathly Hallows*
2009	Anne Carson, *An Oresteia*

Notes

Chapter 1

1 Since the Athenian calendar began in summer, the year can be referred to as 459/8. Since the play was performed late in the year, we know it was in 458.

2 Burnett 1971: 81, 92–3, and see Sommerstein 2008c: 220–3 and Marshall 2014: 79–95.

3 Pickard-Cambridge 1988: 57–91 and Wilson 2000.

4 Marshall and van Willigenburg 2004: 101: 'the nature of the judging procedure means that nothing certain can ever be concluded from how a particular play placed'.

5 This is the case with Michael Suliardus, the scribe of a manuscript in Wolfenbüttel, the Codex Guelfertybanus (Guelf. Gudianus Graecus 88), which preserves correct readings e.g. at *LB* 944 and 1046; see West 1990: 356.

6 Murray 1914, Kott 1967, and Kerrigan 1996: 171–92 provide some influential statements.

7 Pickard-Cambridge 1988: 93–5, and see *Vita* 15.

8 Garvie 2009: ix–xxii, and see Rosenbloom 1993 and Harrison 2000.

9 Gantz 1980.

10 Garvie 2009: liii–lvii.

11 See *TrGF* (vol. 1) poets 12, 13, and 24 (= Snell 1986: 88–89, 139–42).

12 See, in favour of a post-Aeschylean date, Bees 1993, who does not press the connection with Euphorion. Sommerstein 2010a: 16n. 15 raises a possibility I find compelling, that the two plays, *Prometheus Bound* and *Unbound*, were presented as a dilogy at the Lenaia (this is then incompatible with the possibility that it was with *Prometheus* that Euphorion defeated Euripides at the Dionysia in 431; cf. 2010a: 29).

13 This last passage is corrupt (see Sommerstein 2008b: 203 n.346, whose translation I provide) but the verbal echo is clear regardless.

14 "The word *dikē*, and words derived from it, are used obsessively in the
   Oresteia to gloss the narrative of revenge" (Goldhill 2004: 28, and see
   28–33); see also Sommerstein 2010c: 193-203.

15 Ostwald 1986: 28–53, Wallace 1989: 72–93, Rhodes 1992: 67–77. For
   Aeschylus, see also Macleod 1982: 127–9.

16 See also Aristotle, *Ath. Pol.* ('The Athenian Constitution') 25.4, Diodorus
   of Sicily 11.77.6, and Plutarch, *Pericles* 10.8; Sommerstein 2010a: 156–9.

17 Collard 2002: xlii.

18 Goldhill 2004: 24–33 and 81–4, Mitchell-Boyask 2009: 97–107.

19 Wiles 1997: 69–86. Some scholars deny the presence of a physical altar,
   but if there was nothing, then a temporary (prop) altar would be placed
   at this point when needed. In *Libation Bearers*, certainly, there was a
   marker representing a tomb in the *orchēstra*.

20 Marshall 2003 considers various castings, and see Knox 1972: 109 for
   the 'voice of Apollo'.

21 West 1990: 268–9 suggests movable painted panels to indicate precise
   locations was possible for the *Oresteia*. This to me seems much less
   likely, and if this were standard, we would expect to see more scene-
   shifting in the extant plays.

22 Thiercy 1986: 19–89, Padel 1990: 354–65. For a proposed connection
   between the *skēnē* as a place where unspeakable rites take place and the
   killings in *Agamemnon* and *Libation Bearers*, see Sourvinou-Inwood
   2003: 246–50.

23 Dover 1966.

24 If the mention of three huts in a lost comedy by Eupolis (fr. 48) were
   known to describe the stage setting of that play, that would be a
   post-458 use, but one passage without context is not enough to decide
   the issue for *Libation Bearers*.

25 The roof is not used in *Libation Bearers*, but it is available, and was
   probably the location from which the Watchman spoke the opening
   lines of *Agamemnon* (*Ag.* 1–39).

26 See Hughes 2006 for an Athenian vase *c.* 420, which I have argued
   depicts the prologue of a satyr play (Marshall 2014: 161–3); fourth-
   century vase-painting from South Italy regularly depicts a low platform.

27 In spite of this, I continue to use the terms onstage (= in the

performance area, and normally in view of the audience) and offstage (= not in the performance area).

28 Poe 1989, Ley 2007: 46–69.

29 Rehm 1988, Scully 1996.

30 Note that the three principal contentions argued in this section are also argued by Garvie 1986: *thymelē* (xliii–xliv) and the single door (xlvi–lii), where he presents a position contrary to that adopted here, and role assignment (xlix, liii–liv) which is different but not incompatible. These are issues of genuine scholarly controversy, and while they will change specific staging decisions, only occasionally do they impact the further analysis of the play.

31 Wiles 1997: 133–74, and see Aronson 2004 for the theatrical function of the door.

32 See Prag 1985: 68–94, Garvie 1986: ix–xxvi, Gantz 1993: 676–86.

33 Goldhill 2004: 46, and see 41–7.

34 Sommerstein 2010c: 136–45.

35 West 2013: 244–87, esp. 282–4.

36 Garvie 1970: 87–8, 1986: xiv–xv.

37 Garvie 1986: xvii–xxii, and see Davies and Finglass 2014: 157–62, 482–511.

38 Garvie 1986: xix–xxi

39 Information about this poem comes from a variety of later sources: the scholia to Euripides, *Orestes* 46 (fr. 216); *P.Oxy.* 2506 fr. 26 ii; and see scholia to Euripides, *Orestes* 268 (fr. 217); scholia to *LB* 733 (fr. 218); Plutarch, *Moralia* 555a (fr. 219).

40 Finglass 2007: 5–19 remains undecided. Garvie 1986: xxiv–xxv prefers 474; Kurke 2013 argues for 454.

41 Garvie 1986: xii–xiii, xv–xvii, xxii–xxiv, Gantz 1993: 677–9.

42 Paris, Louvre, MNB 906.

43 See Prag 1985: 11–13 and 136–7 (Foce de Sele), 10 and 136 (Olympia), 51–6 and 146–7 (Melos). The dating of the Melian reliefs is very uncertain; see Appendix, items 12–16.

44 *ARV*^{2} 652 = Boston 63.1246; see Prag 1985: 3–4, 23–6, 135 and 141. Vermeule 1966 argues that the vase responds directly to Aeschylus' plays of 458. This is possible but unlikely, and cannot be demonstrated by

direct comparison. One would expect greater prominence to be given to Clytaemestra if direct allusion to Aeschylus were intended.

45 Gantz 1993: 680.

46 Winnington-Ingram 1983: 136, and see Garvie 1986: xxxi–xxxiii.

47 Pickard-Cambridge 1988: 1–25, and see Hamilton 1992, Bowie 1993: 22–4, and Parker 2005: 290–326.

48 Pickard-Cambridge 1988: 10.

49 Pickard-Cambridge 1988: 15–16.

Chapter 2

1 *LB* 1–3 (from *Frogs* 1126–8), 3a–b (*Frogs* 1141–3), 4–5 (*Frogs* 1172–3), 6–7 (scholia to Pindar, *Pythian* 4.145), 8–9 (scholia to Euripdes, *Alcestis* 768). West 1990: 229–33 convincingly inserts lines 3a–b into what had been an established sequence. See Bowen 1986: 26.

2 Sommerstein 2010a: 11–29, esp. 15–16.

3 Pickard-Cambridge 1988: 67–8.

4 Wiles 1988: 83.

5 Marshall 2014: 202–4.

6 Taplin 1978: 122–39, with discussion of the *Oresteia* at 122–7. He does not consider the opening in terms of mirror scenes, but see 1978: 35–6.

7 Bowen 1986: 27.

8 Garvie 1970: 85–6.

9 Taplin 1977: 334 discusses many character pairs in tragedy, where only one figure speaks.

10 Scullion 1994: 71–4 and see Chapter 3.3.

11 Taplin 1977: 337n. 1

12 Sommerstein 2008b: 213.

13 Sommerstein 2008c: 224–33. The play apparently featured a pregnant Semele and the goddess Hera.

14 Taplin 1977: 334–6 suggests hiding near the *skēnē* (i.e. upstage), followed by Wiles 1988: 83.

15 Plutarch, *Mor.* 46b and Athenaeus 1.21d–22a.

16 Hermann moved line 165 to the beginning of this speech.

17 Another verbal echo between these passages is in the description of Orestes as an exile (*Ag.* 1282 *pheugas, LB* 136 *pheugōn*).

18 Sommerstein 2010a: 190–1.

19 Wiles 1988: 83, adding 'Earth is subsequently required for the discovery of footprints'.

20 I follow the scholia reading *xiphē* (sword) in 163, for the manuscript's *belē* (missile, weapon); see Sommerstein 2010b: 108–9.

21 Wiles 1988: 84.

22 This would also create a visual echo of the removal of Agamemnon's boots (*Ag.* 944–7).

23 See Appendix, items 1–9 and 12–16, and McPhee 1986 and Dennert 2009.

24 Sommerstein 2008b: 241.

25 Fraenkel 1950: iii 815–26, following with small variation earlier scholars beginning with Schütz, and see Bowen 1986: 177–81.

26 Garvie 1988: 66 accepts the incongruity, with the weaving being part of Orestes' costume.

27 Vidal-Naquet 1981.

28 Garvie 1986: 111.

29 Vellacott claims 'the long speech (269–305) ... mentions neither justice, nor the need to cleanse his house, nor the city's welfare' (1977: 115), but as we shall see both the *oikos* and *polis* are present in the concluding lines. The emphasis, admittedly, is on Orestes' personal hardship.

30 Again, textual corruption affects this passage, but the line order of Hartung, moving 276–7 between 274 and 275, yields the best sense and is widely accepted. Burnett 1998: 106 n.28 argues to keep the manuscript line order.

31 Sommerstein 2008b: 248 n.62 connects it with the disease *leukē* (Aristotle, *Historia Animalium* 518a12–13 and [Aristotle] *On Colours* 797b14–16).

32 West, following Stanley and Dobree, suggests a short (one-line) lacuna immediately following line 284. *LB* 285 does not make sense in the received text. The line was deleted by H. L. Ahrens (a choice accepted by Sommerstein), and moved after 288 by Blomfield and Hermann.

33 Bowen 1986: 68.

34 Rosenmeyer 1982: 337.

35 Newiger 1961: 427–30.

36 Bain 1977: 111–13, Biles 2007.

37 Taplin 1977: 341–2, discussing the source of the corruption at
   LB 713, believes it arises from a subsequent producer wishing to
   make the opening more spectacular, through the addition of extra
   bodies. Marshall 2001 suggests an axe was used as the weapon to kill
   Agamemnon in reperformance, in contrast to the sword used in 458.

38 Dio of Prusa (Dio Chrysostom), *Or.* 52 and 59, provides a direct
   comparison of the three playwrights' *Philoctetes* plays, of which only the
   last, Sophocles' play of 409, is extant.

39 See Torrance 2013: 13–62 for an overview of Euripidean engagement
   with the *Oresteia*.

40 In what follows I present the barest of summaries, treating the plays
   in their production order as I understand it. Nothing changes with
   different proposed dates, except for the possibility that Sophocles'
   Electra is a very early play, in which case it would be responding to the
   original *Oresteia* production. This is very unlikely.

41 Aristotle, *Poetics* 16, 1454b 25–7, notes that even the scar in the *Odyssey*
   was used to effect recognitions of different qualities.

42 Similarly, Andromache's entrance on a wagon at Euripides, *Trojan
   Women* 568 creates a visual echo with Agamemnon's entry in a
   chariot, with the boy Astyanax serving as a prominent counterpoint to
   Aeschylus' Cassandra.

43 In the past forty years, Bain 1977 and Kovacs 1989 argue for deletion;
   Hammond 1984, Davies 1998, and Gallagher 2003 for retention, all
   using different lines of argumentation.

44 See Appendix, item 2, and Coo 2013 for indications that a fourth-
   century vase painter conflated the two sensible sisters in his depiction of
   the recognition scene.

45 Segal 1966, Ringer 1998.

46 Eur. *El.* 1252–3 predict the Erinyes in Orestes' future, but not in the
   action of the play. The Erinyes are part of the subsequent punishment of
   Orestes in *IT* and *Or.*

47 Gantz 1993: 681–83.

48 Pickard-Cambridge 1988: 41 n.3.

49 Hall similarly suggests, 'In my view it is likely that by the fourth century, at least, the first play was often dropped from performances of *Libation Bearers* and *Eumenides*, whether separately or together . . .' (2005: 60).

50 Pickard-Cambridge 1988: 99–100.

51 Kerrigan 1996: 145–69.

52 The full title: *A New Interlude of Vice, Containing the History of Horestes, with the cruel revengment of his father's death upon his one natural mother.* See Pickering 1962 for a facsimile edition of the play and Knapp 1973.

53 Kerrigan 1996: 170–92.

54 Ewbank 2005: 39–40. With these cuts, Agamemnon never appears in *Agamemnon*, but the Watchman, the *parodos*, Clytaemestra's beacon speech, and Cassandra's lyric are preserved, but nothing else.

55 Glasson 1948 details resonances between *LB* and *Macbeth*.

56 Hall and Macintosh 2005: 462–87, Macintosh 2005: 294.

57 It was performed by the Theatro Technis of Karolos Koun (Athens, 1945), and the Classical Theatre of Oregon (1995), and was featured at Ancient Drama Festivals in Syracuse (1921, 1978, 1996, 2001), Epidauros (1987), Pisa (1997), Majorca (1997), and Elea (2007), among others.

58 There have been a substantial number of school and university productions of *Libation Bearers*, most of which are in translation. These include including American Academy of Dramatic Arts (1908), Manchester (1912), Newbury Grammar School (1915), UCLA (1933) Agnes Scott College in Atlanta (1935), Sorbonne (1949) Washington (1950), Potiers (pre-1952), Hull (1969), Otago (1971), JACT Summer School (1987), University College London (1992) Newcastle (1993), Detroit Mercy (1995), Portland State (1995), King's College London (1999), Randolph-Macon Women's College (2002), Catholic University of America (2004) and Oxford (2011). This is a partial list, drawn from the Database of the Archive of Performance of Greek and Roman Drama at the University of Oxford.

59 This is admittedly a rough measure, but since the script was published (Sheppard 1933, identified as the same text as was used in the 1921 production) and was intended to be used as a crib during performance, it is possible to be precise. Not unexpectedly, the *kommos* in particular was reduced.

60 Foley 2012: 233–4. See Hartigan 1995: 76–9 and Foley 2005. The first use of this three-author trilogy appears to be at the 1930 Festival of Ancient Drama in Syracuse, Sicily.

61 Rich 1992. For this production see also Bethune 1993, Goetch 1993 and Salter 1994, Hartigan 1995: 79–80, and de la Combe 2005. Bethune describes why many felt *Eumenides* was an anticlimax after the end of *Libation Bearers*: the first three plays 'were prepared over a period of some thirty weeks, at which point, as she said, "The money ran out and we had to start performing." It was a year later that the fourth play, *The Eumenides*, was prepared over a period of some three months. There is a clear difference between the last play and the other three …' (1993: 186).

62 Taplin 2002: 10–11, and see Macintosh 2005: 311–21. Hartigan 1995: 68–81 discusses American productions. Foley 2012: 12–26 ('American Electra') examines a range of modern performances and adaptations of the story, and the exclusion of Aeschylus in the performance tradition is notable.

63 Burian 1997: 254–61.

64 Foley 2012: 14–17, and see Weiner 2013 for a different classical connection.

65 Burian 1997: 267, Reynolds 2005: 136–8.

66 Stodelle 1984: 183–99.

Chapter 3

1 See Foley 2003 for an excellent overview of the chorus.

2 This is suggested by a scholion to Euripides, *Hecuba* 647.

3 Wilson 1999.

4 Taplin 1977: 338.

5 Conacher 1987: 103, and see 108–13.

6 Reinhardt 1949: 114–15, 119, and see 110–40.

7 Conacher 1987: 109, and see Lesky 1943: 118–21, Lebeck 1971: 110–30.

8 Greek numbers are used to label passages: Αα (1), Ββ (2), Γγ (3), Δδ (4), Εε (5), Ζζ (6), Ηη (7), Θθ (8), Ιι (9), Κκ (10), Λλ (11).

9 This accepts Schütz's proposed transposition of *LB* 434–8 to follow 455.

10 Garvie 1986: xxxiii.

11 *LB* 151 similarly presents 'a paean for the dead man'; *Ag.* 645 a 'paean to the Erinyes'.

12 Scott 1985: 90

13 E.g. Garvie 1986: 157–8, Scott 1985: 90–3 and 202–4 notes 95–9.

14 The note in Page's 1972 Greek text is far too absolute: ... *manifesto perperam, quamvis mirus sit stropharum ordo* ... ('clearly wrong, though the order of strophes is marvelous').

15 Wilamowitz 1914: 205–10 and Lesky 1943.

16 'Left here (in their proper place), they interfere with his view that at this point Orestes was still struggling with his conscience over the mother-murder' (Conacher 1987: 132 n.32; cf. Lloyd-Jones 1979: 34, Collard 2002: 177, etc.) Sier 1988: 52–179, esp. 155–8, instead reverses the order of the first two speeches, which yields bAc | CaB (he also assumes Orestes speaks 418–22, saying 'mother' and throwing off the rhythm of the earlier pattern). They create another unparalleled but easily interpretable pattern for the original audience, but leads to other problems (see Sommerstein 2010b: 110 n.75)

17 Sommerstein 2008b: 267 n.98 and 2010b: 109–13. The proposal is anonymous, but predates 1955.

18 See Rogers 2017.

19 Text: Harrison 2002: 1–182. Performed by the National Theatre, in the Olivier Theatre, with music by Harrison Birtwhistle and designs by Jocelyn Herbert. A recording was made and broadcast on Britain's Channel 4 in 1983 (see Wrigley 2012), but is no longer commercially available from the distributor, Films for the Humanities. For discussions of this production, see Parker 1986, Taplin 2002, and 2005.

20 Performed by the Barnard Columbia Ancient Drama Group, 3–5 April 2014, at the Minor Latham playhouse. Recording available online (barnardcollege 2015).

21 Sommerstein 2008b: 275.

22 This accepts Ludwig's deletion of *LB* 505–7, a version of which is cited by Clement of Alexandria as coming from Sophocles. See Garvie 1986: 174, 182–3, and Sommerstein 2008b: 276–7 n.112.

23 *Persians*: Lawson 1934. *Psychagogoi*: Rusten 1982, Bardel 2005: 85–92,

Cousin 2005, and Sommerstein 2008c: 268–73. There is an Attic red-figure volute krater, *c.* 480 BCE, which shows a chorus dancing and apparently invoking a ghost: Basel, Antiken-museum und Sammlung Ludwig BS 415 (Hart 2010: 29).

24 Sommerstein 1980: 67–9, 2010c: 128. Rosenmeyer 1982: 248: 'The appeal in *Libation-Bearers* is truly necromantic . . . In the end, Agamemnon does not appear'.

25 Sommerstein 1980: 67.

26 Budelmann, Maguire, and Teasdale 2016 consider different ways that ambiguity works in drama, with examples from *Libation Bearers* and other plays.

27 There are some textual issues with this passage, but they do not affect this interpretation. West's proposal to exchange the positions of lines 528 and 534 is unusual, but produces a text that reads smoothly and may be correct (1990: 245–6).

28 Agamemnon interprets his own dream, incorrectly, at *Iliad* 2.1–75. This pattern points to the weirdness of *Odyssey* 19.535–53, where Penelope's dream interprets itself.

29 For snake-imagery in the tetralogy, see also *Ag.* 1233; *LB* 527–50, 994, 1047, 1050, and Whallon 1958.

30 Does this indirectly anticipate that Pylades will eventually speak in this play? I do not think it does, except in retrospect: it is rather a theatrical conceit and reminder that the man who has been onstage since the play begins could speak if he wanted; he is simply the strong, silent type.

31 Prag 1985: 10–34, 136–43. The iconography persists after the *Oresteia*, too: e.g. Louvre K320, an Apulian (South-Italian) *oinochoē*.

32 Burian 1986.

33 Garvie 1970: 85–6.

34 Bowie 1993: 16–18.

35 Stinton 1979 and see Conacher 1987: 116–17.

36 Lebeck 1967: 183.

37 The absence of swords in some post-458 vase illustrations (Sommerstein 2010c: 163–4) does not necessarily reflect stage practice, given that the interest of these scenes is on an earlier moment of the play.

38 Taplin 1977: 338–42; 'the lyric snaps the moorings of locale and setting . . .' (Rehm 1994: 95).

39 Exactly this assignment of space is presented uproblematically in Murray's 1923 translation: 'In Aeschylus' time, there was probably no actual change made in the stage arrangements. The back wall represented a palace front, while in the center of the orchestra was an altar or mound which stood for Agamemnon's tomb. In the first half of the play you attended to the tomb and ignored the back scene: in the second you attended to the castle and ignored the mound' (1923: 78).

40 Collard 2002: 67; cf. Sommerstein 2008b: 287, 297.

41 Garvie 1986: 197. We should not assume the actor subsequently speaks the Attic words with a drawl or accent to suggest Phocian foreignness.

42 Marshall 2014: 222–5, 285–9.

43 Scullion 1994: 71–4

44 Taplin 1978: 122 and see 122–39 and Garvie 1986: xxxv–xxxviii. Taplin does not discuss this example, and his mirrors will be considered in Chapter 4.

45 *Libation Bearers* therefore has the exact same location (with the *skēnē* representing the House of Atreus) as the previous play. Had this happened before in Greek drama? We know of no other plays where spatial direct continuity from one play to the next would exist (it is unlikely to emerge in a tetralogy not narratively linked).

46 Brown believes door-knocking 'should not be seen as an intrinsically comic device' (2000: 2).

47 Taplin 1977: 299–300, 306–8, 316–17; 1978: 33–5.

48 See Sommerstein 2010a: 151 for the time of arrival.

49 *Ag.* 1538–40; *Ag.* 1397–8 anticipated this moment allusively as a mixing bowl filled with wine, and see *LB* 491.

50 *Xen-*: 657, 662, 668, 674, 680, 684, 700, 702, 703 (twice), 710 (and see Sommerstein 1980: 69–70). *Phil-*: 656, 683, 695, 705, 708, 717.

51 Taplin 1977: 342. In the same way, *Eum.* 405 preserves a memory of a performance variant in which Athena entered in a chariot.

52 My sense is that if this is a variation from a subsequent performance, then it is from the fourth century, since the extant tragic receptions in Sophocles and Euripides do not show Orestes and Pylades heavily attended.

53 Taplin 1977: 340. The closest parallel to this for the discarding of a prominent character is the noble self-sacrifice of the maiden in

Euripides' *Children of Heracles*, who offers herself to be killed, but the narrative shifts without a posthumous recognition of her death.

54 Budelmann, Maguire, and Teasdale 2016: 93–8.

55 Gantz 1993: 680. The parenthesis is telling.

56 Thomson 1966: ii 161–5, Winnington-Ingram 1983: 216–18, Seaford 1989.

57 Seaford 1989.

58 I use the designation A, B, and C because in 458 the terms protagonist, deuteragonist and tritagonist (first, second and third actor), if they were in use at all, did not indicate a hierarchy or priority in the way they are often used today (a separate competition for actors emerged later, *c.* 449).

59 Marshall 2003.

60 See Chapter 4.1; if actor C plays Cilissa, the feeding of the infant Orestes is obscured since both characters share body and voice; actor B is also possible, creating a connection between Electra and Orestes' infant nurture.

61 Similarly, in Euripides' *Hecuba* (*c.* 421), the servant sent with a message at *Hec.* 609–11 returns being played by one of the speaking actors at 658.

62 Gantz 1993: 683.

63 Another possibility, that Electra returns at 668 but does not speak lines 691–9, or is the Doorkeeper, provides no theatrical benefit that I can perceive.

Chapter 4

1 Marshall 2017.

2 Marshall 2014: 229–32.

3 Garvie 1986: 259.

4 Winnington-Ingram 1983: 221–2, following Wilamowitz.

5 Rosenmeyer 1982: 232: 'Orestes has the heart of Perseus naturally within him'.

6 Rosenmeyer 1982: 218: 'Aegisthus has the bearing of a tired,

small-minded administrator. He claims to be grief-stricken but his skepticism concerning the news shows that he wants it to be firm'.

7 Schadewalt 1932: 321 n.1. The cry *e e* is also found in the manuscript reading of *LB* 790 (chorus), but both Sommerstein and West accept Weil's emendation *aie*.

8 Sommerstein 2010c: 156–7.

9 *LB* 10 Chorus onstage; 584 Electra off; 684 Clytaemestra (and Electra?) on; 718 Orestes, Pylades, Clytaemestra (and Electra?) off; 730 Cilissa on; 854 Aegisthus off.

10 Compare Admetus' instructions to a servant detailing the inside of his house, at Euripides, *Alcestis* 546–50.

11 Sommerstein 2010a: 151–3, who notes that following her nightmare the previous evening, this is the second night in a row that Clytaemestra has been awakened. *Rhesus*, a tragedy by an unknown author that survives among the plays of Euripides, is also set at night.

12 Sommerstein writes, 'she may give the impression of having dressed hurriedly, perhaps wearing only her inner garment (*chiton*) without the overgarment (*himation*) and/or with dishevelled hair' (2010c: 160).

13 This line is adapted by Sophocles, *Electra* 1478–9.

14 Hamilton 1978: 70–1.

15 Garvie 1986: 291: 'The pathos of Clytaemestra's words contrasts strikingly with Orestes' tone … Unimpressive as we know him [Aegisthus] to be, he was still loved by Clytemnestra. It is a side of her that hardly emerged in *Ag*'.

16 O'Neill 1998, Marshall 2017.

17 In later plays, Clytaemestra has babies with Aegisthus, but that is not explicit here (Gantz 1993: 683–4).

18 Conceivably, the verb *ethrepsa* could mean 'raised from infancy' rather than 'wet-nursed', but that's an odd distinction for her to draw.

19 Whallon 1958: 274.

20 Burnett 1998: 112 n.48 rightly mocks the decorum urged in discussions of staging this moment.

21 Taplin 1972: 79–80.

22 Knox 1979: 53 n.10: 'There is ample time for a change of costume.'

23 For this much-discussed scene, see Easterling 1973 on the presentation of Agamemnon's gullibility, and Taplin 1977: 308–16 on the staging.

24 See also *LB* 148 'victory-bringing Justice' (*Dikēi nikephorōi*), and 890, where Cytaemestra says 'Let us see if we win or are defeated' (*eidōmen ei nikōmen ē nikōmetha*).

25 See Appendix, items 10 and 11; item 17 presents a related image in silver.

26 Line assignments are always to be suspected, and it is possible *LB* 929 was spoken by Orestes, a final couplet to close the scene, as indicated in M.

27 This is the interpretation of the scholia, and cf. Euripides, *Orestes* 1400–2.

28 The word *miastōr*, to cite the standard Greek-English lexicon, means a 'crime-stained wretch who pollutes others' (LSJ). Also found at *Eum.* 177, it is apparently the converse of *alastōr*, a spirit of righteous revenge (cf. *Ag.* 1501, 1508).

29 Also, in *Eumenides*, Athena's role emphasizes that she is daughter of Zeus and no other (*Eum.* 736–8), even if her sense of justice is to be questioned.

30 Sophocles' *Ajax* 430–3 derives the hero's name Aias from the cry *aiai*, and Pentheus in Euripides' *Bacchae* 367–8 is cognate with suffering (*penthos*).

31 Murray 1923: 79. Rosenmeyer 1982: 217: 'She, too, has her share of comedy, though she is not as such a comic person. Like the watchman [in *Ag.*], she is oppressed by the weight of the immediate, and fails to recognize larger issues. Personal loyalty, nostalgia, and even sentimentality control her thoughts'.

32 The alternative, that he is employing a fourth speaking actor for a brief role of three crucial and momentous lines only, does not reduce the unusual nature of this theatrical moment.

33 Again, even if more than one door were available, their unique use in tragedy in this scene would mark *Libation Bearers* as even more unusual in this respect.

34 This resonates with the supposed realism of Euripidean tragedy, and will be confirmed later in the play when Aeschylus gives an example

of a Euripidean monody in which a woman has lost her pet rooster (1331–64). The generalization, especially as a contrast to Aeschylus, is not accurate.

35 Similarly, at *Frogs* 1063–4 Aristophanes' Aeschylus accuses Euripides of introducing royal figures in rags (making reference in the first instance to *Telephus* in 438), even though exactly that happens in *Persians* (472).

36 De Quincey 2006 [orig. 1823]: 3.

37 De Quincey 2006: 5. On the same page, he elaborates: 'in the murderer, such a murderer as a poet will condescend to, there must be raging some great storm of passion … which will create a hell within him'.

38 De Quincey 2006: 6.

39 Burnett 1998: 111.

40 Murray 1923: 82.

41 The availability of the *ekkyklēma* in 458 has been doubted (Taplin 1977: 442–3), and Taplin believes mute extras carried the bodies into view (1977: 357). I believe it was employed from the earliest days of the *skēnē*, but this cannot be proved. What is important is the visual echo with *Agamemnon*, revealing an interior scene and used to make a symbolically powerful entrance. We do not know the dimensions of the cart, its height, the size of the wheels, or the noise involved when it rolled, but only with such a device can all spectators see the *tableau* without slowing the action to bring the bodies onstage.

42 Taplin 1977: 357–9, 1978: 124–6.

43 The net imagery appears to predate Aeschylus, and is seen on the vase by the Dokimasia painter (*ARV²* 652 = Boston 63. 1246; see Chapter 1.4).

44 Sommerstein 2010c: 158–9.

45 Again, manuscript corruption slightly obscures this point, as an intrusive line (986) which identifies the 'father' as Helios the sun has been introduced to the manuscripts. I accept Barrett's deletion, with West and Sommerstein 2010c: 153. Further, West suggests introducing a lone Aeschylean line, fr. 375 'and display the device that made him helpless' (tr. Sommerstein; from a scholion to Euripides, *Orestes* 25) that would further describe the cloth, between 983 and 984, yielding the following sequence: … 982, 983, 983a, 984, 985, 987, 988 … . (West 1990: 232, 262–3).

46 Fraenkel 1950: iii 809–15 argued that lines 991–6, 1005–6, and 1028 were the product of a later reperformance (not necessarily the one in the 420s), but an actor's interpolation; see also Lloyd-Jones 1961, Bowen 1986: 182–4, Sommerstein 2010b: 116–17.

47 See Brown 1983: 15–20.

48 Sommerstein 2010a: 192–3, 2010c: 130.

49 The speech, too, is corrupt. See Sommerstein 2010b: 117–18.

50 It may also be a continuation of the wrestling imagery at *LB* 866–8 (Larmour 1999: 125–6; my thanks to Jonathan Vickers for this observation).

51 Similarly, Banquo in *Macbeth*, Act 3, Scene 4, appears as a ghost perceived by the audience and Macbeth but not by others on stage.

52 Brown 1983: 19–20.

53 Whallon 1980: 88–99 and 1995; see Brown 1983: 13. Whallon wants Erinyes onstage in *Agamemnon* as well, perched like vultures in the *skēnē* roof. That is not what I am suggesting, and would remove the surprise effect here.

54 It is from this number that attendants, silent slaves, etc. will have been drawn for the fuller scenes in *Agamemnon*.

55 Mnouchkine's *Les Atrides* had this moment as a highlight: 'the most extraordinary *coup de théâtre* … arrives after the blood is spilled: as the lights dim to black and the barking of approaching dogs rises to a terrifying pitch, individual attempts to remove the bloodied mattress bearing the mutilated corpses of Clytemnestra and her lover, Aegisthus, come to nothing' (Rich 1992).

56 Collard 2002: xlvii n. 30 suggests it may come from much later in antiquity, perhaps originating outside Athens.

Appendix

1   Vases with the death of Agamemnon, as in *Agamemnon*, or Orestes seeking sanctuary at Delphi, drawing on *Eumenides*, are not included here; see Prag 1985: 1–5, 44–60, 134–5, 143–8. Coo 2013: 87–8 lists scenes predating *Libation Bearers*.

2 It does not follow from this that other vases depicting an attendant are to be understood as presenting Chrysothemis.

3 E.g. Robinson 1932.

4 Prag 1985: 10–34, 85–94, 109–14, 136–43 (and plates 6–21), and see Vermuele 1966.

Bibliography

Aellen, C., A. Cambitoglou and J. Chamay (1986), *Le peintre de Darius et son milieu: Vases grecs d'Italie méridionale*. Geneva: Association Hellas et Roma.

Aronson, Arnold (2004), 'Their Exits and Their Entrances: Getting a Handle on Doors', *NTQ* 20: 331–40.

Bain, David (1977), '[Euripides], *Electra* 518–44', *BICS* 24: 104–16.

Bardel, R. (2005), 'Spectral Traces: Ghosts in Tragic Fragments', in F. McHardy, J. Robson and D. Harvey (eds), *Lost Dramas of Classical Athens*. Exeter, 83–112.

Barlow, Jane A. and John E. Coleman (1979), 'Orestes and Electra at Cornell', *AJA* 83: 219–25.

barnardcollege (2015), 'Aeschylus' Choephoroi ("Libation Bearers") (2014)', *Youtube*. Available online: https://www.youtube.com/ watch?v=i05l02aNtnA (accessed 6 March 2017).

Bees, R. (1993), *Zur Datierung des Proetheus Desmotes*. Stuttgart.

Bethune, Robert (1993), 'Le Théâtre du Soleil's *Les Atrides*', *Asian Theatre Journal* 10: 179–90.

Biles, Zachary P. (2006–7), 'Aeschylus' Afterlife Performance by Decree in 5th C. Athens?', *ICS* 31–2: 206–42.

Bowen. A. (1986), *Aeschylus: Choephori*. Bristol.

Bowie, Angus (1993), 'Religion and Politics in Aeschylus' *Oresteia*', *CQ* 43: 10–31.

Brown, A. L. (1983), 'The Erinyes in the *Oresteia*: Real Life, the Supernatural, and the Stage', *JHS* 103: 13–34.

Brown, P. G. (2000), 'Knocking at the Door in Fifth-century Greek Tragedy', in S. Gödde and T. Heinze (eds), *Skenika: Beitrage zum antiken Theater und seiner Rezeption*. Darmstadt: Wissenschaftliche Buchgesellschaft, 1–16.

Budelmann, Felix, Laurie Maguire and Ben Teasdale (2016), 'Ambiguity and Audience Response', *Arion* 23.3 (Winter): 89–114.

Burian, Peter (1986), '*Zeus Sotēr Tritos* and some Tiads in Aeschylus' *Oresteia*', *AJP* 107: 332–42.

Burian, Peter (1997), 'Tragedy adapted for stages and screens: the Renaissance to the present', in P. E. Easterling (ed.), *The Cambridge Companion to Greek Tragedy*. Cambridge: Cambridge University Press, 178–208.

Burnett, Anne Pippin (1971), *Catastrophe Survived: Euripides' Plays of Mixed Reversal*. Oxford: Clarendon Press.

Burnett, Anne Pippin (1998), *Revenge in Attic and Later Tragedy*. Berkeley: University of California Press.

Collard, Christopher (2002), *Aeschylus:* Oresteia. Oxford: Oxford University Press.

Conacher, D. J. (1987), *Aeschylus'* Oresteia*: A Literary Commentary*. Toronto.

Coo, Lyndsay (2013), 'A Sophoclean Slip: Mistaken Identity and Tragic Allusion on the Exeter Pelike', *BICS* 56: 66–88.

Cousin, C. (2005), 'La *Nékuia* homérique et les fragments des *Evocateurs d'âmes* d'Eschyle', *Gaia* 9: 137–52.

Davies, M. (1998), 'Euripides' *Electra*: The Recognition Scene Again', *CQ* 48: 389–403.

Davies, M. and P. J. Finglass (2014), *Stesichorus: The Poems*. Cambridge: Cambridge University Press.

De La Combe, Pierre Judet (2005), 'Ariane Mnouchkine and the History of the French *Agamemnon*', in F. Macintosh et al. (eds), *Agamemnon in Performance, 458 BC to AD 2004*. Oxford: Oxford University Press, 273–89

De Quincey, Thomas (2006), *On Murder*. Oxford: Oxford University Press [includes 'On the Knocking at the Gate in *Macbeth*', *London Magazine* 8 (October 1823) 353–6, at 2006: 3–7.]

Dennert, Martin (2009a), 'Elektra I', *LIMC* Supp. 2009.1: 193–5.

Dennert, Martin (2009b), 'Elektra I', *LIMC* Supp. 2009.2: 95–6.

Dover, K. J. (1966). 'The *skēnē* of Aristophanes', *PCPS* 192: 2–17.

Easterling, P. E. (1973), 'Presentation of Character in Aeschylus', *G&R* 20: 3–19.

Easterling, P. E. (ed.) (1997), *The Cambridge Companion to Greek Tragedy*. Cambridge: Cambridge University Press.

Ewbank, Inga-Stina (2005), '"Striking too short at Greeks": The Transmission of Agamemnon to the English Renaissance Stage', in F. Macintosh et al. (eds), *Agamemnon in Performance, 458 BC to AD 2004*. Oxford: Oxford University Press, 3752.

Fagles, Robert (1975), *Aeschylus: The Oresteia*. New York: Penguin Books.

Finglass, P. J. (2007), *Pindar: Pythian Eleven*. Cambridge: Cambridge University Press.

Foley, Helene (2003), 'Choral Identity in Greek Tragedy', *CP* 98: 1–30.

Foley, Helene (2005), 'The Millennium Project: Agamemnon in the United States', in F. Macintosh et al. (eds), *Agamemnon in Performance, 458 BC to AD 2004*. Oxford: Oxford University Press, 307–42.

Foley, Helene (2012), *Reimagining Greek Tragedy on the American Stage*. Berkeley: University of California Press.

Fowler, Barbara Hughes (1969), 'Aeschylus' Imagery', *C&M* 28: 1–74.

Fraenkel, Eduard (1950), *Aeschylus: Agamemnon*. 3 vols. Oxford: Clarendon Press.

Gallagher, Robert L. (2003), 'Making the stronger argument the weaker: Euripides, *Electra* 518-44', *CQ* 53: 401–15.

Gantz, Timothy (1980), 'The Aischylean Tetralogy: Attested and Conjectured Groups', *AJP* 101: 133–64.

Gantz, Timothy (1993), *Early Greek Myth: A Guide to Literary and Artistic Sources*. Baltimore: Johns Hopkins University Press.

Garvie, A. F. (1970), 'The Opening of the *Choephori*', *BICS* 17: 79–91.

Garvie, A. F. (1986), *Aeschylus: Choephori*. Oxford: Clarendon Press.

Garvie, A. F. (2009), *Aeschylus: Persae*. Oxford: Oxford University Press.

Goetsch, Sallie (1994), 'Playing against the Text: *Les Atrides* and the History of Reading Aeschylus', *TDR* 38.3: 75–95.

Goldhill, Simon (1984), *Language, Sexuality, Narrative: the* Oresteia. Cambridge: Cambridge University Press.

Goldhill, Simon. (2004), *Aeschylus. The Oresteia*. 2nd edn. Cambridge.

Goldman, Hetty (1910), 'The *Oresteia* of Aeschylus as Illustrated by Greek Vase-Painting', *HSCP* 21: 111–59.

Goward, Barbara (2005), *Aeschylus: Agamemnon*. London.

Glasson, T. Francis (1948), 'Did Shakespeare Read Aeschylus?', *London Quarterly and Holborn Review* 173: 57–66

Griffith, M. (1995), 'Brilliant Dynasts: Power and Politics in the *Oresteia*', *Classical Antiquity* 14: 62–129.

Hall, Edith (2005), 'Aeschylus' Clytemnestra versus her Senecan Tradition', in F. Macintosh et al., *Agamemnon in Performance, 458 BC to AD 2004*. Oxford: Oxford University Press, 53–75.

Hall, Edith and Fiona Macintosh (2005), *Greek Tragedy and the British Theatre 1660–1914*. Oxford: Oxford University Press.

Hamilton, Richard (1978), 'Announced Entrances in Greek Tragedy', *HSCP* 82: 63–82

Hamilton, Richard (1992), *Choes and Anthesteria: Athenian Iconography and Ritual*. Ann Arbor: University of Michigan Press.

Hammond, N. G. L. (1984), 'Spectacle and Parody in Euripides' *Electra*', *GRBS* 25: 373–87.

Harrison, Thomas (2000), *The Emptiness of Asia: Aeschylus' Persians and the history of the fifth century*. London: Duckworth.

Harrison, Tony (2002), *Plays 4: The Oresteia, The Common Chorus (Parts I and II)*. London: Faber.

Hart, Mary Louise (2010), *The Art of Ancient Greek Theatre*. Malibu: Getty Publications.

Hartigan, Karelisa V. (1995), *Greek Tragedy on the American Stage: Ancient drama in the Commercial Theater, 1882–1994*. Westport, CT: Greenwood Press.

Hughes, A. (2006), 'The "Perseus Dance" Vase Revisited', *OJA* 25: 413–33.

Hughes, Ted (1999), *The Oresteia of Aeschylus: A New Translation*. New York: Farrar, Strauss, and Giroux.

Jacobsthal, P. (1931), *Die Melischen Reliefs*. Berlin.

Kerrigan, John. (1996), *Revenge Tragedy: Aeschylus to Armageddon*. Oxford: Clarendon Press.

Knapp, Robert S. (1973), '*Horestes*: The Uses of Revenge', *ELH* 40: 205–20.

Knox, B. M. W. (1972), 'Aeschylus and the Third Actor', *AJP* 93: 104–24. Reprinted in B. Knox (1979), *Word and Action: Essays on the Ancient Theatre*. Baltimore: Johns Hopkins University Press, 39–55.

Kossatz-Deissmann, A. (1978), *Dramen des Aischylos auf Westgriechischen Vasen*. Maintz.

Kott, Jan (1967), 'Hamlet and Orestes', *PMLA* 82: 303–13.

Kovacs, David (1989), 'Euripides, *Electra* 518–44: Further Doubts about Genuineness', *BICS* 36: 67–78.

Kurke, Leslie (2013), 'Pindar's Pythian 11 and the *Oresteia*: Contestatory Ritual Poetics in the 5th c. BCE', *Classical Antiquity* 32: 101–75.

Larmour, D. (1999), *Stage and Stadium*. Hildesheim: Wiedmann.

Lattimore, Richmond (2013), *Aeschylus II: The Oresteia*. 3rd edn. Chicago: Chicago University Press.

Lawson, J. (1934), 'The Evocation of Darius (Aesch. *Persae* 607–93)', *CQ* 28: 79–89.

Lebeck, Anne (1967), 'The First Stasimon of Aeschylus' *Choephori*: Myth and Mirror Image', *CP* 62. 182–5.

Lebeck, Anne (1971), *The Oresteia: A Study in Language and Structure*. Washington, DC: Center for Hellenic Studies.

Lefkowitz, Mary and James Romm (2016), *The Greek Plays*. New York: Modern Library.

Lesky, Albin (1943), *Der Kommos der Choephoren*. Vienna.

Ley, Graham (2007), *The Theatricality of Greek Tragedy: Playing Space and Chorus*. Chicago: University of Chicago Press.

Lloyd-Jones, Hugh (1961), 'Some Alleged Interpolations in Aeschylus' *Choephori* and Euripides' *Electra*', *CQ* 11: 171–84.

Lloyd-Jones, Hugh. (1979), *The Choephoroe*. London: Duckworth.

Macintosh, Fiona (1997), 'Tragedy in Performance: Nineteenth- and Twentieth-century Productions', in P. E. Easterling (ed.), *The Cambridge Companion to Greek Tragedy*. Cambridge: Cambridge University Press, 284–323.

Macintosh, Fiona, Pantelis Michelakis, Edith Hall and Oliver Taplin (2005), *Agamemnon in Performance, 458 BC to AD 2004*. Oxford: Oxford University Press.

Macleod, Colin (1982), 'Politics and the *Oresteia*', *JHS* 102: 122–44.

Marshall, C. W. (2001), 'The Next Time Agamemnon Died', *CW* 95: 59–63.

Marshall, C. W. (2003), 'Casting the *Oresteia*', *CJ* 98: 257–74.

Marshall, C. W. (2014), *The Structure and Performance of Euripides' Helen*. Cambridge.

Marshall, C. W. (2017), "Breastfeeding in Greek Literature and Thought," *ICS* (forthcoming).

Marshall, C. W. and Stephanie van Willigenburg (2004), 'Judging Athenian Dramatic Competitions', *JHS* 124: 90–107.

McPhee, Ian (1986), 'Elektra I', *LIMC* III.1: 709–19, III.2: 543–9.

Meineck, Peter (1998), *Aeschylus: Oresteia*. Indianapolis: Hackett.

Mitchell-Boyask, Robin (2009), *Aeschylus: Eumenides*. London.

Morizot, Yvette (1992), 'Klytaimestra', *LIMC* VI.1: 72–81, VI.2: 35–8.

Murray, Gilbert (1914), *Hamlet and Orestes: A Study in Traditional Types*. New York: Oxford University Press.

Murray, Gilbert (1923), *Aeschylus: The Choephoroe*. London: George Allen and Unwin.

Newiger, Hans Joachim (1961), 'Elektra in Aristophanes' *Wolken*', *Hermes* 89: 422–30.

O'Neill, K. (1998), 'Aeschylus, Homer, and the Serpent at the Breast', *Phoenix* 52: 216–29.

Ostwald, M. (1986), *From Popular Sovereignty to the Sovereignty of Law*. Berkeley: University of California Press.

Padel, R. (1990), 'Making Space Speak', in F. I. Zeitlin and J. J. Winkler (eds), *Nothing to Do with Dionysos? Athenian Drama in its Social Context*. Princeton, 336–65.

Page, Denys (1972), *Aeschyli Septem Quae Supersunt Tragoiedias*. Oxford: Oxford University Press.

Parker, R. B. (1986), 'The National Theatre's *Oresteia* 1981–2', in M. Cropp, E. Fantham, S. Scully (eds), *Greek Tragedy and its Legacy: Essays Presented to D. J. Conacher*. Calgary: University of Calgary Press, 337–57.

Parker, R. B. (2005). *Polytheism and Society at Athens*. Oxford: Oxford University Press.

Pickard-Cambridge, Arthur (1988). *The Dramatic Festivals of Athens*, 2nd edn, rev. J. Gould and D. M. Lewis with a new supp. Oxford: Oxford University Press.

Pickering, John (1962), *The Interlude of Vice (Horestes)*. Oxford: Malone Society Reprints.

Poe, J. P. (1989). 'The Altar in the Fifth-Century Theatre', *Classical Antiquity* 8: 116–39.

Prag, A. J. N. W. (1985). *The Oresteia: Iconographic and Narrative Tradition.* Warminster: Aris and Phillips.

Rehm, Rush (1988), 'The Staging of Suppliant Plays', *GRBS* 29: 263–307.

Rehm, Rush (1994), *Greek Tragic Theatre.* London: Methuen.

Reinhardt, Karl (1949), *Aischylos als Regisseur und Theologe.* Bern: A. Franke.

Reynolds, Margaret (2005), 'Agamemnon: Speaking the Unspeakable', in F. Macintosh et al. (eds), *Agamemnon in Performance, 458 BC to AD 2004.* Oxford: Oxford University Press, 119–38.

Rhodes, P. J. (1992), 'The Athenian Revolution', in D. M. Lewis, John Boardman, J. K. Davies and M. Ostwald (eds), *The Cambridge Ancient History*, 2nd edn, vol. V. *The Fifth Century B.C.* Cambridge: Cambridge University Press, 62–95.

Rich, Frank (1992), 'Taking the Stage to Some of its Extremes', *New York Times* (6 October). Available online: http://www.nytimes. com/1992/10/06/theater/review-theater-les-atrides-taking-the-stage-to-some-of-its-extremes.html?pagewanted=all (accessed 6 March 2017).

Ringer, Mark (1998), *Electra and the Empty Urn. Metatheater and Role Playing in Sophocles.* Chapel Hill: The University of North Carolina Press.

Robinson, David M. (1932), 'Illustrations of Aeschylus' Choephoroi and of a Satyr-Play on Hydrias by the Niobid Painter', *AJA* 36: 401–7.

Rogers, Brett M. (2017), 'Orestes and the Half-Blood Prince: Ghosts of Aeschylus in the *Harry Potter* Series', in *Classical Traditions in Modern Fantasy.* Oxford: Oxford University Press, 209–32.

Rosenbloom, D. (1993), 'Shouting "Fire" in a Crowded Theater: Phrynichus' *Capture of Miletus* and the Politics of Fear in Early Attic Theater', *Philologus* 137: 159–96.

Rosenmeyer, Thomas G. (1982), *The Art of Aeschylus.* Berkeley: University of California Press.

Rusten, J. S. (1982), 'The Aeschylean Avernus. Notes on P. Köln 3.125', *ZPE* 45: 33–8.

Salter, Denis (1993), 'Hand Eye Mind Soul: Théâtre du Soleil's *Les Atrides*', *Theater* 24: 59–65.

Schadewalt, W. (1932), 'Der *Kommos* in Aischylos' *Choephoren*', *Hermes* 67: 312–4.

Scott, W. C. (1985), *Musical Design in Aeschylean Theatre*. Hanover, NH: University Press of New England.

Scullion, Scott (1994), *Three Studies in Athenian Dramaturgy*. Stuttgart: Teubner.

Scully, Stephen (1996), 'Orchestra and Stage in Euripides' *Suppliant Women*', *Arion* 4.1: 61–84.

Seaford, Richard (1989), 'The Attribution of *Choephoroi* 691–9', *CQ* 39:302–6.

Segal, Charles Paul (1966), 'The *Electra* of Sophocles', *TAPA* 97: 473–545.

Shapiro, Alan and Peter Burian (2003), *The Oresteia*. Oxford: Oxford University Press.

Sheppard, J. T. (1933), *The Oresteia of Aeschylus*. Cambridge: Bowes and Bowes.

Sier, K. (1988), *Die lyrischen Partien der* Choephoren *des Aischylos*. Stuttgart: Franz Steiner.

Snell, Bruno (1986), *Tragicorum Graecorum Fragmenta*, vol. 1, *editio correctior et addendis aucta*. Göttingen: Vandenhokeck & Ruprecht.

Sommerstein, Alan H. (1980), 'Notes on the *Oresteia*', *BICS* 27: 63–75.

Sommerstein, Alan H. (2008a), *Aeschylus I. Persians, Seven Against Thebes, Suppliants, Prometheus Bound*. Cambridge, MA.

Sommerstein, Alan H. (2008b), *Aeschylus II. Oresteia. Agamemnon, Libation-Bearers, Eumenides*. Cambridge, MA.

Sommerstein, Alan H. (2008c), *Aeschylus III. Fragments*. Cambridge, MA.

Sommerstein, Alan H. (2010a), *The Tangled Ways of Zeus, and Other Studies In and Around Greek Tragedy*. Oxford.

Sommerstein, Alan H. (2010b), 'Textual and Other Notes on Aeschylus (Part 2)', *Prometheus* 36: 97–122.

Sommerstein, Alan H. (2010c), *Aeschylean Tragedy*. 2nd edn . London: Duckworth.

Sourvinou-Inwood, Christiane (2003), *Tragedy and Athenian Religion*. Lanham, MD: Lexington.

Stinton, T. C. W. (1979), 'The First Stasimon of Aeschylus' *Choephori*', *CQ* 29: 252–62.

Stodelle, Ernestine (1984), *Deep Song: The Dance Story of Martha Graham*. New York: Schirmer Books.

Taplin, Oliver (1972), 'Aeschylean Silences and Silences in Aeschylus', *HSCP* 76: 57–97.

Taplin, Oliver (1977), *The Stagecraft of Aeschylus: The Dramatic Use of Exits and Entrances in Greek Tragedy*. Oxford: Clarendon Press.

Taplin, Oliver (1978), *Greek Tragedy in Action*. London: Methuen.

Taplin, Oliver (2002), 'An Academic in the Rehearsal Room', in J. Barsby (ed.), *Greek and Roman Drama: Translation and Performance*. Stuttgart: Metzler, 7–22.

Taplin, Oliver (2005), 'The Harrison Version: "So long ago that it's become a song?"' in F. Macintosh et al. (eds), *Agamemnon in Performance, 458 BC to AD 2004*. Oxford: Oxford University Press, 235–51.

Taplin, Oliver (2007), *Pots and Plays: Interactions Between Tragedy and Greek Vase-painting of the Fourth Century B.C.* Malibu: Getty Publications.

Thiercy, P. (1986), *Aristophane: fiction et dramaturgie*. Paris.

Thomson, George (1966), *The Oresteia of Aeschylus*. 2 vols, new edn. Amsterdam: Hakkert.

Torrance, Isabelle (2013), *Metapoetry in Euripides*. Oxford: Oxford University Press.

Vellacott, Philip (1973), *The Oresteian Trilogy*. Harmondsworth: Penguin Books.

Vermeule, Emily (1966), 'The Boston Oresteia Krater', *AJA* 70: 1–22, 215

Vidal-Naquet, P. (1981), 'Hunting and Sacrifice in Aeschylus' *Oresteia*', in J. P. Vernant and P. Vidal-Naquet (eds), *Tragedy and Myth in Ancient Greece*, trans. Janet Lloyd. New York: Zone Books, 150–74.

Wallace, R. W. (1989), *The Areopagos Council, to 307 B.C.* Baltimore: Johns Hopkins University Press.

Weiner, Jesse (2013), 'O'Neill's *Aeneid*: Virgilian Allusion in *Mourning Becomes Electra*', *IJCT* 20: 41–60.

Whallon, William (1958), 'The Serpent and the Breast', *TAPA* 89: 271–5.

Whallon, William. (1980), *Problem and Spectacle: Problems in the* Oresteia. Heidelberg.

Whallon, William. (1995), 'The Furies in *Choe*. and *Ag*', *CQ* 45: 231–2.

West, Martin L. (1990), *Studies in Aeschylus*. Stuttgart: Teubner.

West, Martin L. (1991), *Aeschyli Choephoroe*. Stuttgart: Teubner.

West, Martin L. (2013), *The Epic Cycle: A Commentary on the Lost Troy Epics*. Oxford: Oxford Universiy Press.

Wilamowitz-Moellendorff, Ulrich von (1914), *Aischylos Interpretationen*. Berlin: Weidmann.

Wiles, David (1988), 'The Staging of the Recognition Scene in the *Choephoroi*', *CQ* 38: 82–5.

Wiles, David (1997), *Tragedy in Athens: Performance Space and Theatrical Meaning*. Cambridge: Cambridge University Press.

Wilson, P. (1999), 'The *aulos* in Athens', in . Goldhill and R. Osborne (eds), *Performance Culture and Athenian Democracy*, Cambridge, 58–95.

Wilson, P. (2000), *The Athenian Institution of the Khoregia: The Chorus, the City and the Stage*. Cambridge.

Winnington-Ingram, R. P. (1983), *Studies in Aeschylus*. Cambridge: Cambridge University Press.

Wrigley, Amanda (2012), 'Greek Plays: the National Theatre's *The Oresteia* (Channel 4)', *Screen Plays* (blog). Available online: https://screenplaystv. wordpress.com/2012/01/23/oresteia-channel-4-1983/ (accessed 6 March 2017).

Zeitlin, Froma I. (1965), 'The Motif of Corrupted Sacrifice in Aeschylus' *Oresteia*', *TAPA* 96:463–508.

Zeitlin, Froma I. (1978), 'The Dynamics of Misogyny: Myth and Mythmaking in the *Oresteia*', *Arethusa* 11: 149–84.

Index

www.ingramcontent.com/pod-product-compliance
Ingram Content Group UK Ltd.
Pitfield, Milton Keynes, MK11 3LW, UK
UKHW020735280225
455688UK00012B/667